OH JOE!

OH JOE!

A Father's Struggle
To Survive The Loss Of His Son

Joseph E. LeBlanc, Jr.

iUniverse, Inc.

New York Lincoln Shanghai

OH JOE!
A Father's Struggle To Survive The Loss Of His Son

iUniverse, Inc.

For information address:
iUniverse, Inc.
2021 Pine Lake Road, Suite 100
Lincoln, NE 68512
www.iuniverse.com

ISBN: 0-595-29666-1 (pbk)
ISBN: 0-595-66032-0 (cloth)

Printed in the United States of America

To Joe,
for all you gave us in years too few,
for all of us you took with you,
Oh Joe!

(March 4, 1971-June 28, 2002)

Contents

In Memoriam

LeBlanc III

Joseph E. LeBlanc, III, 31, passed away June 28, 2002 in Houston, Texas from complications of cystic fibrosis. He was born March 4, 1971 in Baton Rouge, Louisiana to Peggy and Joseph E. LeBlanc, Jr. Joe graduated from LSU in 1998 with a Masters Degree in Exercise Physiology and Cardiac Rehabilitation and was employed by Bally Total Fitness in Houston. He is survived by his loving family, parents Peggy and Joseph E. LeBlanc, Jr., brother Mark LeBlanc and his wife Michelle, grandmother Geraldine Parsons McIndoe and her husband Robert, Joe's fiancée Karen Klein and numerous relatives and friends.

Houston Chronicle, Monday, July 1, 2002

Joseph E. LeBlanc III

Joseph E. LeBlanc III, a personal trainer at Bally Total Fitness in Texas, died Friday of complications of cystic fibrosis in Methodist Hospital in Houston. He was 31. Mr. LeBlanc was born in Baton Rouge and lived in New Orleans for 27 years before moving to Houston four years ago. He graduated from St. Martin's Episcopal School in Metairie. He earned a master's degree in exercise physiology and cardiac rehabilitation from Louisiana State University. Survivors include his fiancée Karen Klein; his father, Joseph E. LeBlanc, Jr.; his mother, Peggy LeBlanc; a brother, Mark LeBlanc; and a grandparent, Geraldine Parsons McIndoe.

New Orleans Times Picayune, Monday, July 1, 2002

Oh Joe!

My son, Joe, has died. On June 28, 2002. My beautiful, beautiful son. I am lost. Words fail me. Emotions overwhelm me, all so confusing but one—the suffocating pain that sweeps over me. And the sadness. I am drowning. I am dying. How can I go on? How can I not? If anything I have ever told Joe is true, I must. But Joe, I need your help. I cannot do it alone. Please, son, reach to me. Help me. Hold me as I so often held you.

This is not a story of Joe's life, though it is a story that needs telling. It is not a recounting of his illness and death. I do not set out to chronicle the events of our lives together or times past. I begin when Joe entered the hospital and go from there. This is a journey through my heart and soul. I have tried to record my feelings and thoughts as they have come to me. And the pain, sometimes in waves, at times all at once, sometimes hard to identify or find words for, but I have tried. I made notes of them as soon as they were felt even without the time to compose. Each dated, saved until later, enough jotted down to capture the thought, the feeling, the searing sense of loss, and the hurt. I wrote them in script as brief or as profuse as I needed to give content and substance enough to write them later in lyrics and poem. I wrote to preserve the feeling so that I could reconstruct it and feel it again. I want these feelings to live on. I felt such urgency to grab hold when they came, before they could be lost or deconstructed by the ravages—or blessings?—of Time, lost in that void of the past just beyond my reach, not even the jottings enough to call them back. I recorded them all and, now at last, write them here.

I cannot begin this journey without a look back. There is so much to see. There was so much life lived by Joe and by us with him. Two things I wrote long ago when Joe was young stand out. They are found in another book I have written, *Defining Moments*. What I write here cannot be complete without them.

"There was another time, shortly after Mark was born, when, reflecting on my two sons and my responsibility to them, I thought of what I would tell them, what I would want them to know about the life that awaited them. What attitudes, what outlooks, what understanding did I have to give them? What had I learned to pass on? What could I say to prepare them for the good and the bad they would see? I could not protect them forever. My truest gift would be to give them a way of life to live.

My Sons

In these your first moments alone,
not yet aware
you are you
or I me,
how I long to counsel you
of life as it impends,
in my fertile hopes for you
the relic age
proclaims its infant truth,
newly freed, in all its sureness,
from all that failed
the many like you come before,
but there will be
time enough for this,
my gift to you now, my sons,
is this:

Do not be consumed
by those for whom
life has but an ugly face
and weeps only labored tears,
nor shaken by the unmasked vengeance
of a world lost faith in itself,
for they will carry on

staggered by the burden
of their unknown loss,

You, my sons, be more,
see beauty where to others eyes
none abounds,
look with compassion
upon those whose spirit
has been more sorely tried
than yours,
and find in every senseless
hated act you cannot accept,
its author's desperate plea
that you understand,
see in every life,
no less than in your own,
that to love,
and you will breathe
your final breath as your first,
with the virgin innocence
you now sigh.

—January 1974

"One day when Joe was young, playing, pretending to be this hero or that, I asked, "Who will you be today?" He said plaintively, almost wistfully, "No one, I'm just Joe." It took me by surprise, and made me realize just how much that was, how much I treasured him being Joe.

Just Joe

Who will you be today?
do you want to play?
or did I hear you say,
"I'm just Joe."

You are Joe,
but not just Joe,
you are the world to come,
here and now,
face to face with itself,
the hopes and prophesies of all
given one more chance in you,
and the world will never
smile at itself,
or cry for itself,
or think of itself
as you again.
You are everything to be
that you will,
and whatever you become,
it will never be again.

Oh,
how the world and I
are enriched because
you're Joe.

—July 1976"

And now Joe is gone. But Joe, oh, how the world and I have been enriched because you were here. And I will never smile, or cry, or think of myself, the same again.

There is also something I wrote to Joe and Mark several years ago as part of a work entitled, *The Bible and Catholic Belief*. My purpose was to summarize for them the Bible basis for the fundamental tenets of the Catholic faith. In the preface, I shared with them some of my thoughts about the human condition and its relationship to what I believe is the saving message of Jesus Christ. I tried to address certain objections often brought up today to question the place of faith and belief in God in "modern times." This is what I told them:

"1. Some say men and women today are too "sophisticated" and "know too much" to believe in unseen Gods and miracles. Yet, I think we need only look about—at the frenetic pace of life, the forced smiles, the vacant stares, and the constant drive to acquire more and more because nothing is ever enough—to see that faith in God is more relevant than ever. We must have a clear sense of where we are going and why, rather than just careening through life at the mercy of goals laid out by others who have no pretense of our best interests at heart.

2. There is a tendency to question the reality of the "divine" by insisting upon an explanation in terms of the physical laws of nature and verification by some form of the scientific method. Since it cannot be explained by the known mechanics of the world as we know it or empirically confirmed, the divine is dismissed as pure "fancy" and "delusion" not worthy of belief by "thinking" and "reasoning" persons. Too often, there is derision and ridicule of those who believe. This is what the sophistication of modern man has wrought. And yet, so much remains the same. This attitude is not a product of modern times. The same doubts were had at the time of Christ. (1 Corinthians 1: 18-31; 2: 1-16; 3: 18-23). They were just as empty then.

There is also the paradox that if something is truly "divine", by definition it cannot be explained in "human" or "natural" terms. It cannot be reduced to the defined principles of our discovered world. Otherwise, it would not be "divine". Thus, it is the essential nature of the "divine" that it cannot be fully explained by known physical laws. Lack of verification is no argument at all against acceptance of the mysteries of faith. The question is whether there must be more than what we can see or measure. It is now widely recognized in the fields of physics and astronomy that there is. If we are able to so readily accept the existence of yet-unidentified states of matter and the possibility of unknown life in other galaxies, why are so many so ready to question belief and faith in God and the heavens?

3. What, then, is behind our search for the "divine"? It is this: What is only human and natural and physical is not enough. It may seem so for a time. But not for long. Not forever. A void remains. An emptiness of spirit. An incompleteness. There must be more. Were this not so, we would not constantly long for something beyond the world around us. Something to give more meaning to what we do than the society-driven, peer-pressured reasons why we do it. We would not wonder so about why we are here, what is our purpose, what are we to do, what is the point of anything, of everything. What we see about us cannot be all there is. There must be more significance to life than this. This wonderment and angst has its roots in what I believe is the fundamental truth of our existence: Our meaning is to be found only in our relationship with the God who made us. Our purpose must come from him. It preceded us and awaits us. We might see ourselves as extensions of God who have been given a choice whether to reunite with him. Life is the process of making that choice. Our understanding of this relationship does not come easy. We must work. And look. It will be worth the effort. Can we ask for any

greater promise than, "Seek and you shall find"? (Matthew 7: 7-8; and Luke 11: 9). How much more assurance do we need?

4. There is another aspect to the search that I need mention: We have a tendency to seek out the God that we want in place of the God who has revealed himself to us through Jesus Christ. We wish for a God who will give us permission, who will grant our wishes, who will favor us in one way or another. We want a God who will make life easier and assist us in our pursuit of wealth and fame and accolades. Any other God we may treat as irrelevant or outmoded or not responsive to the "reality" of the "modern world". In this sense, we are not unlike the chief priests and elders, the scribes and the Pharisees, who rejected Christ when he lived. He did not fit who they wanted the Messiah to be: a king, a leader of nations, a source of power. They would not accept anything less, and certainly not a God whose eye and ear were turned to the poor and the afflicted and the persecuted. Are we any less demanding now of the God we insist upon, or any less rejecting of Christ when he is not the kind of God we want? We must take care not to dismiss or marginalize God because he does not suit who we would choose him to be. We must not yield to the temptation to replace him with our own God.

5. What, then, is the promise of this God who has revealed himself to us in the person of Jesus Christ? Not that all will be good, for it will not. Christ showed us this as He himself suffered and grieved and felt anger and despair. But He showed us much more, and it is there that we find his promise: It is that no matter how bad life may become, He offers the strength to survive and the promise that, if we hold out to the end, we will end well. We are loved. It is a promise of hope and triumph if we will embrace it. If we will have faith.

6. There are those who would reject this promise. They say, "What kind of God would allow such suffering and hardship in the world?" Stated another way in a popular book, "Why do bad things happen to good people?" This, I believe, is the wrong question. Life and the world are random. Once created, they have been placed in our hands, and we are an imperfect people who, for better or worse, have the free will to choose right and wrong, good and bad. If there were not this choice, if all were good and evil non-existent, it would be heaven. We are promised such a place. But not now. Not here. And so the better question is, "What kind of God would abandon those he created in such a world with no hope and no salvation?" Not the God we worship. From the first, this God held out hope and promise through the prophets of old. When it was apparent that his people were not up to the task on their own and more was needed, this God sent his only Son to show how the worst of life can be endured and to re-affirm His promise that there is more. And so the promise lives on.

Our quest goes on for a greater understanding of God as he has revealed himself to us in the person of Jesus Christ. The search is a personal one. It takes place inside and will begin and end with you. For my part, I can only commend these thoughts to you and wish you well. And assure you that, through it all, I am here for you."

The Service

Joe's funeral service was so hard and so moving. The hymns we chose were my favorites: *Ave Maria, How Great Thou Art,* and *Amazing Grace.* The readings we chose did all that readings could do.

The first was from the Book of Wisdom, Chapter 3: 1-8:

> But the souls of the just are in the hand of God, and no torment shall touch them.
>
> They seemed, in the view of the foolish, to be dead; and their passing away was thought an affliction and their going forth from us utter destruction. But they are in peace.
>
> For if before men, indeed, they be punished, yet is their hope full of immortality; chastised a little, they shall be greatly blessed, because God tried them and found them worthy of himself. As gold in the furnace, he proved them, and as sacrificial offerings he took them to himself. In the time of their visitation they shall shine, and shall dart about as sparks through stubble; they shall judge nations and rule over peoples, and the Lord shall be their King forever.

The second reading was from St. Paul's letter to the Romans, Chapter 14: 7-9:

> None of us lives as his own master and none of us dies as his own master. While we live we are responsible to the Lord, and when we die we die as his servants. Both in life and in death we are the Lord's. That is why Christ died and came to life again, that he might be Lord of both the living and the dead.

The third and last reading was from the Gospel of St. John, Chapter 14: 1-6:

> Do not let your hearts be troubled. Have faith in God and faith in me. In my Father's house there are many dwelling places; otherwise, how could I have told you that I was going to prepare a place for you. I am indeed going to prepare a place for you, and then I shall come back to take you with me, that

where I am you also may be. You know the way that leads where I go. "Lord," said Thomas, "we do not know where you are going. How can we know the way?" Jesus told him:

> "I am the way, and the truth, and the life; no one comes to the Father but through me. If you really knew me, you would know my Father also. From this point on you know him; you have seen him.

The priest's words were so comforting and so honest. He stood before the first pew where we were seated and spoke to us in a voice loud enough for all to hear. He said: "I don't know what to say. It's not supposed to be this way. On the one hand—and he stretched out his arm to the right—there are platitudes, and on the other—and he stretched out his other arm to the left—there is silence. And somewhere in between, there is truth, even if we cannot see it now." He went on from there and, through the tears, helped us through the rest of the service until Joe was laid to rest. I have thought often about those outstretched arms and the truth that lies somewhere in between. I must confess, I cannot see it yet. I think it may be that God does not so much reveal His purpose to us as help us to live with it with trust in Him. And so I try. Each day I try. But it is so hard.

After the service, stories of Joe were shared with us, some retold again and others we heard for the first time, another part of Joe left with us. And there were so many cards of condolence. One came several weeks after Joe died and stood out. It read:

> This was no ordinary LIFE. This was a life well-lived and well-loved, a life that will be deeply missed.

Joe's life was, indeed, no ordinary life. It was well-lived and he was well-loved. Joe, you are so deeply missed.

Joe Is Gone

Now it is time to turn to me. Even now, with time passing, it is more than I can imagine. More, it seems, than I can bear. The fear and trembling began when Joe did not recover quickly and leave the hospital that first week or two. So much then began to go unsaid. We hoped, but fear and dread slowly crowded out more and more. We prayed, more and more afraid of what the answered prayer might be. Such conflict. To pray for one thing, but to wonder deep within what is best—something you cannot say out loud. The guilt of thinking such a thought is too much. I do not want to pray for the wrong thing. I must be more loyal and loving than that, wondering all the while, what is love? Who am I praying for? Is it just me trying to hold on?

1.

It became apparent that Joe would not recover and leave the hospital quickly. It was hard to go on with everyday life. I could not pretend this was not happening or that things were normal. There was nothing I could do but wait. I began to do things I had to do, little pieces of time parceled out here and there, but not much more, the minimum of life. Playing for time until our life could be put back together again and Joe would be home, feeling guilt all the while that I was here and he was there. How could I experience joy or happiness? I could not conceive of feeling the emotion. How could I feel joy without Joe, as if to do so would lessen my caring or diminish his role in my life, a role so large that I could not foresee life without him? There can be no joy while Joe is like this.

Guilty
(May 29, 2002)

What am I to do with your smiles,
you out there,
who seem not to know
I am not here,
nothing behind this face to return,
I can only force so much.

Your well-intentioned reaches
are not lost on me,
worse,
at times they appeal,
and I wonder,
how can that be when Joe
has no chance to feel it, too?

How I joyed to see his joy,
emotions he felt, I felt them too,
how can I feel them now
if he cannot feel them, too?

OH JOE!

Lying there,
my emotions are at your side,
yet,
life goes on all about me,
I am in it,
and at times there breaks through
a smile,
and I feel guilty all the while.

2.

I prayed for Joe's recovery as hard as I could, reciting every prayer I knew, voicing every entreaty I could summon. I pleaded, I begged, I mouthed the words rotely. Why would God not answer? Was it asking too much? Christ promised our prayers would be answered, whatever we asked would be granted. Well, I was asking, again and again like the widow God finally answered because she was so persistent in prayer. Still, I received no answers. There was no cure, no recovery for Joe. Why? Were my prayers not enough? Was I not worthy enough? Did my prayers not work because I was not good enough? Did I fail Joe? If I had somehow been better, would my prayers have worked? Could I have saved Joe then? Such visions of grandiosity. They were irrational, I know it. Yet, fleeting though the thoughts may have been, they slipped into my thinking as I sank lower into helplessness.

Worthy
(May 29, 2002)

Where have all my prayers gone?
Were they not delivered,
misplaced somewhere?
How can they not reach a God
who knows them before they are said?

Or was something left undone,
something I said or did
not good enough,
have I been singled out?
Are my prayers the less?

Who am I to pray
whose prayers seem so unheard.
I have no answers,
only wondering and hope,
as I pray and pray again.

3.

My sister was at the hospital with us one weekend. A nurse, she guided us through the charts and numbers with a dialogue no longer found in a health care system that has no time. One day, she and I talked of our parents, both now long gone. As the world around us unraveled, she said, "You know, we're orphans. It's so hard to be orphans at a time like this." She was right. Though we do not think of ourselves that way most of the time, this brings out the child we never left behind who needs its parents now more than ever. We have nowhere to turn. We suffer this alone with each other, but it is not the same. I silently cry out, "Mom! Dad! Please help," and am left with only prayers that so far have not worked. Can they hear me? It is so lonely to be orphaned.

Orphaned
(May 29, 2002)

I look about in distress
in my fear and in my pain,
who have I to turn to
to find comfort again?

Who will hold me and stroke me
and wipe my tears
and assure me there is nothing to fear?
Who will stay with me and wake me
to a new day worth waking to
and assure me the words of hope I hear
still can come true?

So many family and friends gathered near,
but the two needed most no longer here,
there from the first and along the way,
now long gone in those far off days,
and I alone in these shifting sands
left to parent myself as best I can.

OH JOE!

I have gone so long without you,
the memories have had to do,
until now when I need your touch
more than ever to see me through.
Who will feel for me as I feel for Joe,
and stay by my side as I stand at his?
Who will say to me it will be alright
as I say these words to him?

True or not,
how I long for those words,
to feel that embrace,
to hear the world will be safe again
and there is saving grace,
to close my eyes no longer orphaned
and comforted in your care,
missing you more than I can bear.

4.

For several weeks, we stayed at the hotel adjoining the hospital. Early one morning in bed, I thought about all the prayers that were unanswered. I was aware of a resentment toward God, not voiced or consciously admitted, but it was there. Out loud I would say, "There is no point in being mad at God; He's the only game in town." But in the very flipness of those words, it was there—my anger that it was true. Where else had I to go? I tried to force myself to put God and prayer in perspective. I told myself that help and strength come from God and are there for the asking. God knows best. Instead of always seeking favors, I should give thanks for all He has done for me and re-affirm my trust in Him to do what is best for Joe. While I was at it, of course, I asked for Joe's recovery. Above all, I thought, I need to trust and give thanks. After all, God *is* the only game in town. All this was fine in my head. But it could find no place in my heart.

Giving Thanks
(May 30, 2002)

My prayers were not sparing
in their entreaties for Joe,
entrusting all to God's caring
and for God's healing to show,
but more was joined to the asking,
for on the way here
so much had been given,
so much we held dear.

There are thanks to be given
to give God His due,
thanks we did not know
the years left were so few.
He has His way,
I must not forget,
but, granting it all, I must still ask yet:

OH JOE!

Why now? Why Joe?
Why did it have to be Joe?
Must I thank Him even for this
for reasons I cannot know?
What more is there He does not show?

I must believe He cares,
cares for Joe and us all,
and give thanks for the time He gave us
before sounding Joe's call,
and, perhaps, thanks, too,
for what only He can see
was a time ahead not meant to be.

5.

That same early morning at the hotel, I realized all I could do was hope and pray. I could do nothing, change nothing. I was overwhelmed by my helplessness, my son lying there, and I, his father, unable to help. His whole life, I have tried to be there for him. I wanted him to know I would always be there. I think he did and knows it now. I think he understands I would do anything for him if I could, that I love him with all my heart. I know he wants his Dad to take care of him, and I can not.

Helpless
(May 30, 2002)

How can I live with this?
How can I bear it?
My son, lying there,
how I long to protect him
for he is in my care,
needing more from me now
than mere hope and prayer.

But I can only watch,
helpless,
at the mercy of what?
God? Circumstance?
A disease run its course?
What is that to me when
my son is lying there,
and I, his father, unable to act,
helpless,
feeling I have failed.

6.

Some days later, early in the morning at the hotel again, I was so discouraged. All my prayers, all the prayer groups in so many places praying for Joe, and still no recovery. My hope was down. How was this going to change? How will he get better? I was beginning to be afraid to hope anymore. Was I becoming resigned? No! I will not. I will never give up. Without hope, there is nothing. I will hope until every ounce of it is forced from me, and then I will hope for more.

Hoping
(June 2, 2002)

Hoping takes more effort now,
as fear sets in,
not yet dread, not yet said,
but growing despite me,
not better now a worsening.

Time is the enemy,
but still a chance, they say,
those in the know, or so we pray,
and so I hope
even as hope fades,
lying to myself if I must,
I will go down hoping
for I know no other way to live.

7.

That same early morning, I thought again about my unanswered prayers. What more could I do? Then I thought of all the others whose prayers were answered with recovery. What did they do different? Why were their prayers heard and not mine? Was their faith stronger? I do not begrudge them. Still, there is a resentment there, a jealousy, selfish though it is and unjustified, even if I do not admit it. I cannot feel joy for them—it is feigned at best—because I hurt so much. As I walk through the hospital lobby each day, I see patients being discharged, wheeled out in chairs to waiting, smiling family, while upstairs we wait in vain for the slightest sign of improvement, the smallest indication of the hope the doctors say we should have. Then, I think, what greater right do I have to answered prayers? What standing have I to complain? It is for God to decide when and where to answer our call, how He will fulfill His promise to hear us. We are told He will be there for us, in one way or another, to cure or to console and to help us carry on. Somehow I must believe this. I will continue to pray.

Praying
(June 2, 2002)

How am I to pray?
Are my words so different than theirs
that are heard?
Why do you favor their return
to the living and not Joe's?
How did they capture your ear,
and, it seems, your heart,
while you are so deaf to us?

What else can I say?
What more can I do?
Where is your promise to answer me?
The silence is deafening,
or is this your answer,
calling upon me to trust
when no word is heard.

OH JOE!

No word! You say.
You have given me words,
You say.
They need not repeating,
it is left to me to believe them or not,
You say.
What choice do I have?

8.

Later that same morning, a flood of thoughts came over me. I lay thinking of when Joe would recover and return home. What a celebration we would have! This has put everything in such perspective. Not that we did not realize these things before, but we now knew them so much better in our hearts. There will ever be such a sense of urgency about everything. Family is so important. Friends are so needed. They have been so welcome. We will toast them and us and never take for granted again. I cannot wait. I can see it now. We are all laughing.

The Toast
(June 2, 2002)

We are all gathered at table
now that Joe is home,
the hospital a distant past
as we force it farther and farther away,
together to celebrate Joe's return,
as the doctors said he would,
or might or could.

We lift our glasses
and each say our words of thanks,
and listen to his,
treasuring his sound.
Oh, to hear it again!
and I, hoping, praying,
this will come true.

9.

It is the early morning hours at home. We are no longer at the hotel. Joe is sedated and stable, and we go back and forth each day. He is not better, but is not worse. I wonder, as this goes on without improvement, what will happen to make it any easier for him to recover? It seems to me it will only become harder. Still, the doctors insist there is hope. Who are we to say there is not? But it is a strained belief. I am sinking. I think, oddly enough, of Chicken Little screaming, "The sky is falling," and the statement I read somewhere, "We've got to live no matter how many skies have fallen." This is all I know how to do—to brace myself for Life's next assault and throw myself into the breach, reaching for the other side. Rail aimlessly at Life if I will. Rage at the unfairness. But engage. Try. Keep going.

Falling Skies
(June 22, 2002)

What next
will fall from the sky
to unravel my world
another bit at a time?
It was always to be,
but not so soon, not now,
but when?
When will it happen again?

Time does not bargain,
it comes at its appointed hour,
no messenger ahead,
no warning or quarter given,
and so we wait,
bracing for Life's next twist of fate,
but not timid,
fearing to do the least,
waiting for the worst.

OH JOE!

What Life will do
it will do soon enough,
do not rush its time
or withdraw from Life out of rhyme,
it will take us before we know,
long before we are ready to go,
and so until that fateful day when,
let us go forth and live Life full until the end,
not shrinking from an impending pall,
but living no matter how many skies may fall.

10.

Joe has died. On June 28, 2002. It is less than two weeks later. It is, once again, the early morning hours in bed. All I can think is, "Why now?" I seem to have moved past "Why," but why this day, this month, this year? Why not next year or ten years from now? In my head, I can say it could have been last year, or last month, or any time in the past, but it was not. It is now, and I do not understand why it had to be. Why could Joe not have had more time and we more time with him? He was to be married in less than two weeks. He had just moved into his new house four months earlier. We had moved to Houston less than a year ago to be near Joe and Mark. I know we should be thankful for the thirty-one years of Joe we had, but all I can think or feel now is that he is gone. We have no more time with him. There is no future. The past will console us soon enough. For now, there is only pain and loss and hurt, and the wonder: Why now?

Why Now?
(July 9, 2002)

You are gone,
and I search in vain
to understand your passing,
not so much why—
we must all go—
but why now,
with you on the verge of so much,
with so much life demanded from you,
and you took it all in stride.

We began to relax,
the fear began to subside,
you believed it, too.
Did we take too much for granted?

No! Not at all,
We must count that the fear
did subside,
we did start to relax,

we did begin to believe,
this counts for much.

It was a gift
that the approaching end was unknown,
did not announce its coming
to rob any moments but the last,
the rest of Life yours to live as you chose,
and you did,
and we so blessed to be there with you.

11.

Before this, I thought I knew pain. I had suffered the death of my parents, my grandparents, a younger brother when I was four years old, uncles, and aunts. I had known disappointment, but not like this. All else pales before the heartbreak I feel now. Before, I could always imagine life after the loss. Now, I cannot conceive of a world that does not have Joe. I struggle to know how I feel about living in such a world. It takes such effort to go on. Pain and hurt are the only certainties, always there. The sky no longer looks as blue, nor the sun as bright, as they once did. There is a gloom that envelopes me and the world in which I now find myself.

My Pain
(July 15, 2002)

What a lesson in pain
I have learned!
No way to know there was
so much to be taught,
much more than I could imagine.

As dreadful as my fears could seem,
nothing could prepare me for this,
adrift in a world I do not know,
a world suddenly without Joe,
at once familiar and strange and desolate,
feeling my way laden with grief,
feeling little else.

Not like the world before there was Joe,
it was forever changed by him,
carrying his mark,
and what a mark it was,
his every act, his every thought,
every emotion turned loose
continues on,

and I hold tight to them,
it is what he left me,
forever mine.

12.

My faith has been shaken. It is tested as never before. As much as I prayed, and then this. I am left with feeling, "What is the point?" "Why pray?" God will do what He wants anyway. Clearly, I do not have much to say about it. I know—in my head because my heart will not allow it—that prayers are always answered, and sometimes the answer is "No." I must believe there was a reason Joe died now. Perhaps it was that he would never have made a recovery he would have found acceptable. Maybe this saved him from further ravages of the disease. He did go out at the top of his game, not nickeled and dimed to death by the slow, insidious effects of cystic fibrosis. I do not know the reason why. What I do know is that the only way through this heartbreak and loss is through continued faith and trust in God. I cannot imagine any other way. Perhaps there is. I do not say this is true for everyone. But it is true for me. I must believe and hold on. I must believe what I told Joe and Mark about God's promise: If we hold out to the end, we will end well.

My Faith
(July 15, 2002)

When all is done,
every effort made,
no more prayers to be prayed,
nothing more to say,
when all else has failed,
I have only faith left to me,
to renounce or renew,
and to wonder,
has it failed me, too?

What is this faith?
How do I define it?
As prayers answered and wishes granted,
only outcomes that we choose,
conditioned on what we want,
denied if we do not have our way?

Or is it more,
belief despite
the happenings and unravelings
and our choice of answered prayers,
belief in a larger purpose we cannot see,
the maker's design for you and me.
It must be this, or
what, then, can faith be,
but blind belief in
only what we see.

13.

I have spoken about my pain and how it crowds out all else. As I look back on our life with Joe, there was so much good and wonderful. I see that, too. I cannot—I will not—live with just the pain. It will be there and will never go, but it will not be alone. It will share a place with the memories of Joe and us, the celebrations and the joys, the thanks and the gratitude, all that we shared and the sharing we take with us. Let me write about that, too.

Shared Places
(July 15, 2002)

There is a sharing afoot,
for a place and a space in my life,
the pain that has held sway
confronts a lifetime of memories
that will not be kept at bay,
Joe's life not just a measure
of his ending,
but a lifetime lived full and well,
shared with us for us to tell,
a lifetime brimming even as it waned,
with gifts to us that outweigh the pain.

They are coming back, these memories,
but they take their time,
slowly displacing the sadness and grief,
moving at their pace not mine,
but in the end,
the memories will win,
for they are Joe as he lived,
and as he died,
his dying not the death of memories,
but his final gift to us opened wide.

14.

How I loved Joe! For thirty-one years. Of all the emotions that overwhelm me, this is at the heart of them all. This is what hurts the most at his passing. It is also the most enduring. It is what will carry me through. To have loved Joe, to have had his love, is with me always. I am not left with only grief and pain, though there is more than enough of that. Joe has left me his love, and this will help me bear it if I will let it. I must give it a chance.

My Love
(July 15, 2002)

How I loved Joe!
The moment of his birth,
I remember it well,
and the moment of his dying
will live with me as well,
and the years in between,
thirty one in all,
more than we were led to expect
before he was called.

Joe proved them wrong,
and made believers of us, too,
how we loved him,
through all he had to do,
and it was much,
much to bear,
much more than should have been his share,
all borne without complaint,
and we so awed at such restraint.

Such a trove of memories
he left to share,
ever reminding of his care,
assuring me there is not only sorrow and pain,

and that the love we shared lives on the same,
living and loving as we did then,
lasting a lifetime until I see Joe again.

15.

Since Joe died people ask, "How are you doing?" I know you mean well, but I wonder: How do you think I am doing? What answer do you want? What answer do you expect? Is it assurance you seek that everything is alright? I cannot give it. Things are not alright. They are terribly wrong. I cannot say I am doing fine, no matter how much discomfort this may cause. I sometimes want to say, "Which me are you talking to?" Me at work, me with friends, on stage for all in one way or another? Me alone where I cry out loud, not muffled sounds, but wails and groans? Or me the other times I cry inside? This is the me you do not see who does not fare nearly so well as the one on stage. But I am doing better because you ask. You force me to reach out and connect, even if only for show, to go through the motions each day as they become more than that, leading my slow return to the living.

As for how I am doing, I do not know how to answer. Some days I cry less than others. I still manage to get up each morning and put one foot in front of the other and make it through the day. But how am I doing? Not good. I cannot imagine happiness or joy. I just arise each day and go forward and do my best. That is all I know to do. Thank you for asking. Ask again.

How Am I Doing?
(July 16, 2002)

How am I doing?
How do I answer?
Am I to say what I know you want to hear,
consoling words to allay your own fears?
What can you think when you ask?
How would you be doing in my place?

And what if I am not doing well,
if I am sinking and losing ground,
crying out for hope where none is found?
What will you make of that?
Do you really want to know, or
is your asking the safest way to break the silence,

in all its awkwardness,
benign enough to encourage no details?

To answer, though:
I struggle each day,
my mind labors to convince me
this is not a dream, just an illusion,
I grope about to redefine my place in a world
so changed I scarce know it,
I search for meaning and purpose in a world
suddenly devoid of both,
I laugh, I cry, and try to understand
what it all means.

How am I doing?
Not well just now,
but, hopefully, with time
and your friendship and concern,
I will do better.

16.

I sometimes wonder, "What does any of this mean? What am I to make of it?"
The question is wrapped up in "why" and "why now." Is there purpose or mean-
ing to be found, or is it all just random? Am I meant to learn something, to grow
as a person? How does this affect who I am, my sense of place? I know only that
this is altering of everything.

What Does It Mean?
(July 16, 2002)

What am I to make of Joe's dying?
Is there meaning I am meant to find,
a deep understanding to divine?
or am I to accept it blindly,
as what?
God's will?

Is there magic to calling it that,
as if such resignation will sooth
without explanation?
How can I find meaning
when I cannot understand?
Is there only context within my reach,
only perspective to bring me peace?
Soothing words that death comes to all,
diseases run their course and take their toll,
all so lacking,
unanswered, still, is, why Joe? Why now?
It was so sudden.
and always the question, what does it mean?

What does it mean for me?
Am I at risk at any time, and from what?
And for the future,
does uncertainty now loom larger,

fear of the unknown greater,
the specter of randomness threatening
to lessen the point of everything?

No!
They can not detract from now,
let them cheat not the present,
treasure instead the blessing of not knowing
what is to come,
no measuring of moments
as if tragedy is poised to strike.

This is how Joe lived
to the end,
he would have it no other way,
nor must we,
this is the meaning that he sends.

17.

After Joe's funeral, we went to our place on the beach in Destin, Florida. Joe loved it there. He was there just six weeks before he became ill. Standing on the balcony with Mark, overlooking the Gulf, Mark said, "Sometimes it doesn't seem real. Sometimes I think it's like when I used to go days without speaking with Joe, but I knew he was just a phone call away. We just had not spoken on the phone. Sometimes I feel this is like waiting for him to call." I know what Mark meant. It is so unreal. I used to drive to the office in the morning knowing that Joe was at home preparing to leave for work. As I drive to work now, sometimes it seems like Joe could still be there. He is just out of sight. But I know better. I want my old life back with Joe, but it is gone as surely as he is. I do not know what will take its place. What will the world be like without Joe? I cannot imagine. But I will go on, and will be able to because I was blessed to live for thirty-one years in a world with Joe. I am defined by his presence in my life and am so much more for it. I take every experience with him with me as I go. He gave me this and, even now, is always with me. This is what is real.

Is It Real?
(July 15, 2002)

I was there,
at the hospital when Joe passed away,
at the service where the final words were said,
at the cemetery when he was laid to rest
in the place we chose,
places for us set aside on either side of him,
and after, as we gathered at the house,
and later at Joe's home to collect his things,
now returned here to a room upstairs.

Even now, I wonder,
Is it real?
I close my eyes and I see Joe,
feel his hug so huge,
hear his voice, "Hey, Dad,"

OH JOE!

I pass the gym and imagine him inside.
Is it real?

Can it be just a dream?
Will I wake to the world as it was?
Is Joe just not here for now?
Will I turn and see his face
and hear his voice,
and feel his embrace?

Oh, to have this one more time!
I would make it last forever,
never letting go.
He will be back I know,
but we must wait,
wait until we go to him,
when the world or wherever
will be as it was again,
and I, able to live until then,
only because
I am in a world that Joe was in.

18.

The early morning hours are the worst, before the demands of day force themselves upon me and seize my thoughts, before I am occupied with other things. Lying there, drifting, I cannot avoid the awful truth: Joe is gone. Thoughts of Joe sweep over me, waves of sorrow and sadness and regret. This is when they come. When I wake, I can look for purpose and meaning and reflect on prayer. The early morning hours are before that, when all I do is feel. It hurts so much.

The Early Morning Hours
(July 18, 2002)

They are the worst,
these early morning hours,
not yet forced out by the demands of day,
sleep not yet stolen away,
not yet in motion,
interstitial moments of being
where there is nothing but thought,
drifting, wandering, seeking its own level,
driven by emotions,
nowhere to run, nowhere to hide.

Memories intrude,
fears of the day start their haunting,
of what has happened, of what is to come,
nothing to distract or occupy,
a time before having to cope,
a time to let go,
and I do,
and cringe and cry at what has happened to Joe.

The enormity of it all,
unable to occupy myself with any thoughts
but this,
waking to a world without Joe,

OH JOE!

a world I did not choose,
a world I cannot escape or forget.
They are hard, these early morning hours.

19.

The days are long and hard now. They force themselves upon me as I go through the motions of life until the next day, when it starts again. Is tomorrow here already? It is so wearing. Then I think of all Joe did in dealing with his CF. They were things he would rather not have done, but he did them without complaint. This was said so many times at Joe's funeral. My nephew remarked that what always impressed him about Joe—and inspired him—was that Joe never complained. None of Joe's friends at work knew he had CF. They were amazed at what Joe was able to accomplish despite this disease. One said, "I'll never complain about anything again." So I will go on each day and do what must be done, whether wanting to or not. This is what Joe would do. He always did.

Each Day
(July 18, 2002)

The days are long and hard now
since Joe died.
I, not up to new beginnings,
wake only to know he is not here.
Where can I hide?

The covers beckon,
but do not last,
and so I rise from these depths,
doing and saying all the day long,
the doing and saying now all wrong,
until it ends,
bedded down at last,
the darkness approaching,
but here all along,
my last thought before I close,
as my first,
Joe is not here.

OH JOE!

Can I dream him back,
that reverie where wishes can come true,
or is he missing there, too?
I, at the mercy of what will come,
still left searching when night is done.
and then the day,
it starts again,
my wakings without Joe
without end.

20.

It is the early morning hours again, this time in Destin. I lie there, trying to make sense of a world where this could have happened. It is not supposed to be this way. How can I face a world like this? There is no peace to be had with it. Surely, it cannot be part of a plan. What kind of plan would be like this? I do not want to live in a world where this would make sense. I do not want to try to understand it, as if it could be justified or explained. How am I to come to terms with the world that is left? All I can do is try, sifting through the ruins, looking for some sign of life.

Making Sense
(July 19, 2002)

Where am I?
What is this strange, alien place,
so changed, so unknown,
where Joe is not here?

I look for him still,
listen for his coming,
strain to believe he is somewhere near,
to sense his presence,
but I am doomed,
he is gone,
and I am left in a place
I do not know.

Faces, places look the same,
but hollow, vacant,
less there than used to be.
What do they mean
in a world that would leave them
and take Joe?

There is no sense to be had,
no sense to be made of this,

nor do I want a world
where there is.
And so I wander on,
wondering less and less,
surrendering to the pain which
alone makes sense.

21.

I will never get over Joe's death. In time, they say, it will come. Time heals all. The passage of time is God's way of healing us. I can only say there has not been time enough yet. If time will tell, I can only make do until then, waiting silently until some comfort or peace enters my life. It eludes me now, and will, I fear, until Joe and I meet again. Until then, Joe, pray for me, son, watch over me, comfort me as only you can.

Making Do
(July 19, 2002)

There is no getting over this,
Joe's passing.
Speak to me if you will
of Time and healing and going on,
fine words, well intended,
but the wound is too deep,
only so much can be healed,
never enough,
as my spirit limps along,
never upright, never rested,
always trembling,
making do.

22.

I am on my way to work. The sights are familiar, but nothing is the same. My mind drifts. My old life is gone. It left with Joe. There is no way back to the way it was, though I long for it so. How I miss Joe! Everything looks so bleak without him. There is such a sense of foreboding. If it happened before, it could happen again. I am afraid. Lost. How can I go on? What am I to do? Nothing matters as much anymore. There is an emptiness about me. But there is more. There is still Joe and what he left me. His memory. His touch upon my life. In the very loss I feel, he lives on. This gives me the strength to rise each day and try. Motions gone through one day will be more, or so they say. I hope they are right.

Going On
(July 29, 2002)

There is no way back
to what was,
no road to normalcy again,
it is dead and gone with Joe.
Must we start over again?

No! Not at all.
Joe did not live in a vacuum,
nor did we,
we had each other,
he touched so many, not just us,
he was a part of the whole,
and lives on in what is left,
in what he left,
in what he touched.

As we go on,
he goes with us,
this life of his he loosed upon us,
so much of me left with Joe,

OH JOE!

so much of Joe is left with me,
we are together wherever we may be.

23.

Joe, I feel your loss so much. The hurt is consuming. It is everywhere I look, in everything I see. I am lost in a world without you. I want you back. I want our life as it was, not this new world thrust upon me. I will not let you go. The pain I feel is all I have. I cannot give it up. It is my only connection with you, more real than memories. Thoughts are not enough. I need more. I need to feel your presence, and my pain is the only way. I miss you, son. I miss you.

Clenched
(July 30, 2002)

I hold tightly still to Joe,
no loosening of the grip
to relieve the pain,
it is my hold on him
as memories begin to fade,
blurring,
imperceptible now but quickening
I know,
under the fresh imprint of Time.

So long as I hurt,
I feel,
the numbness replaced,
Joe is close,
touching me.
I cannot lose this, too,
he will not be dispatched to memory
as long as I can feel the pain,
and so I huddle here,
my body and my mind unwilling to let go,
still clenched.

24.

It is early morning again. I am alone with my grief. There are family and friends near, all supportive and caring. They have concern for me, I know. I am thankful for them, but I am alone with a hurt only I can know, the loss of what Joe meant to me. It is a loss only I can feel. It is mine, what I am left with when others must tend to losses of their own. I value this aloneness, the solitariness of my sorrow. It is a special connection with Joe just for me, not diluted or shared with others as if to do so would leave less for me. Yet, even as I dwell in my heartbreak, I am grateful for the touch of others to let me know I am not alone. They are there when I am ready for them, when I need them.

In Solitary
(August 5, 2002)

Here I am alone again
with my grief and my sorrow,
a loss all my own.
I can share bits and pieces,
yes,
but always more there
only I can touch,
that only touches me.

My son, my beautiful, beautiful son,
no one knew you as I,
as I did not know you as they,
you, special to each of us,
your leaving a loss only we can bear
alone.

25.

I am driving home from work. Another day gone through. A night's relief ahead, until it starts again. I look about. It is all so familiar. The same drive each day, the same sights and sounds, but nothing is the same. Joe is gone. Nothing will ever be the same again. The sameness is but a cruel illusion ignoring that Joe is no longer here. I resent it so, these efforts to entice me into believing things are not so different. Everyone goes about their way, while all the while I want to scream, "Joe is gone and I will never be the same." I no longer fit in this world of sameness. It is not the same world to me. Where am I to go? There is nowhere. Would I go if I could? I cannot leave a world where Joe was for thirty-one years. He lives on in every person he touched, in every moment he shared, in every emotion he set free upon the rest of us. Once set in motion, he continues on, his life force in me and in you. He is part of this sameness I rail against. He is there to be found, amidst the sights and sounds that were familiar to him and remain familiar to me.

Sameness
(August 5, 2002)

Things look the same,
trees blossom, rain falls,
I see faces known or not,
buildings skylined up and out,
worker bees scurry about,
the hum of life goes on,
my senses betray me sometimes,
seeming to portray a world not so different.

How I resent it so, this sameness!
Nothing is the same
for Joe is gone,
the sameness but a cruel illusion,
thief of my grief and loss.
Liar, liar!

Nothing is the same,
I am not the same.

Or, Sameness,
are you not despot or vandal,
but gentle healer,
careful not to force too much
at once,
preparing me for a world
of change and loss,
easing for me the tragic cost.

26.

They say we do not know our appointed time to end. We cannot choose it. Only God knows the hour and the day. It is His choice and for His reasons. We know only that when it comes, we do not want it to be then. But if not now, when? Who are we to say when the time should be? If we had it to choose, what would our choice be? How could we decide on a day and hour? Death cannot make sense except in the context of God. If we are to hold to this belief, it is His choice.

If Not Now, When?
(August 8, 2002)

Why now was it Joe's time
to go?
But when would I have it be?
Are blessings to be counted
it was not sooner?

We have so little to say
of when,
struggling to put it off,
taking so much for granted,
as well we should,
it is a gift,
and then
holding so fiercely to now
when the gatherer approaches,
trying desperately to fend him off,
bargaining for more time,
when all along
the deal was done,
and we only being told about it
now.

27.

Joe had a place in my life, in all our lives, in the world in which he lived. All I can think now is he is gone. I am left with such emptiness. There is a hole in my life, a weariness of spirit having to face this loss every waking moment. It never leaves me. Then I realize that Joe's place is not gone. Once occupied and filled by him, it can never go. It survives his passing. It cannot be taken back. It is his place forever for me to visit in my mind and in my heart. I go there often. Joe is always waiting, loving me just as when he was here.

Place
(August 10, 2002)

Joe has gone to a better place,
they say.

But what of his place with us?
It did not leave with him,
it was thirty one years in the making
and cannot be undone,
a place made
in my heart and yours,
where he lingers still
and always will.

And what of the place we made with him?
He took this, too,
this part of us, me and you,
to care for us from afar,
til our turn to cross the bar,
watching over us from this better place,
til once again we see his face.

28.

Joe's dying is not the way it was supposed to be. Parents are not meant to bury their children. It is out of order. That is why it is so cataclysmic when it happens. People shy away from speaking of it. It is every parents worst fear. I wonder, is there any order, really, to anything? We are desperate to believe there is, for we must have some measure of predictability to go on. Otherwise, there is nothing but chaos. We cannot have that. But what control do we have? As I survey the ruins of my life, is there any order to what is left? How can I believe there is when this has happened? How can I not fear that it will happen again? How can I count on anything being as it should again? I can only wait and see. The wait now will be so much more fitful and frightful.

Order
(August 10, 2002)

What right have we to speak of order?
What assurance is ours?
We rise and fall in a rhythm of sorts,
a seeming symmetry,
nature behaves,
and will behave this way again,
only to rear its ugly head,
one time this way,
the next, the other,
who can tell?

Joe was not supposed to die,
it was out of order.
Why did life turn on us so?
If this,
is there only chaos?
Nothing to believe,
sentenced to wait

for the sentence passed
to seal our fate.

Or is there unseen order
in this, too,
Life or nature exacting its due,
not out of order for what was done,
but the measure of a time that had come.

29.

I do not think the pain from Joe's death will ever heal. Not really. Not fully. It may lessen, but it will remain, an ever present reminder that nothing is the same. Since it will be here, I must try to find a place for it, a way to include it in what is left of my life. Let it be a part of new dreams I hope to have—dreams that seem distant now, but one day may come. I cannot dwell only on the pain. It will have its place, but there is so much more of Joe's life to celebrate. Celebrate I will. It is just hard right now.

New Dreams
(August 10, 2002)

My dreams seem so distant now
that Joe is gone,
once so clear, so settled,
needing only time to unfold
as we planned,
now, all dashed,
in their wake only pain and loss,
and tears without end.

Will I ever dream again?
I am afraid to hope,
to take Life's dare,
with Life's upper hand now laid bare,
but what is living if I cannot dream?
What is Life if only what it seems?

I must have more,
and so,
armed with all Joe left me of himself,
his strength and his tenderness,
his laughter and his smiles,
I venture out again,
the steps tentative at first,

OH JOE!

I am still on fragile footing,
fears abound,
but the quest begun,
with Joe by my side,
for new dreams.

30.

When I step back from what I must do to get through the day, when I have drawn all the comfort I can from the cards and notes from family and friends, when I have finished with the abstract explanations and neatly-stated rationalizations for Joe's death and the well-intended attempts to understand, when all the usual sources of solace have been spent, when I stop and think, just think, of what has happened, it overwhelms me. It is mind-numbing and shattering, this happening so cruelly forced upon us. Our world is gone. Our hopes and dreams and plans, all gone. I am struck by how close to going our plans are, just an instant away from dashing, this other reality hovering just out of sight. I still cannot believe it is real. Is Joe, too, just out of sight? Could he be just over there? What is over there? What does it matter, if he is not here?

Unreality
(August 10, 2002)

When all have gone,
the well wishes over,
the prayers all said,
the voices quieted,
only the silence of my mind,
it is unreal: Joe cannot have died.

It is not true,
I am someone else,
I am somewhere else,
this did not happen to Joe,
or to me,
the world could not have changed so
in an instant,
otherwise, who is safe?

If only I could sleep,
anything to lose the consciousness,
when I wake it will be different,
sleep will make it go away.

OH JOE!

Where can I hide?
Where will reality not find me?

But find me it will,
and it has,
and the pain is mortal,
already the death of me,
who will I be now?

31.

The pictures are such sweet reminders of Joe. Bittersweet, I should say. We have so many over the years. Joe always liked to look at the pictures of growing up. We stare at them now and how they captured him. Looking is such joy and pain, but the joy outweighs the hurt. What laughter and tears, but the laughter outlasts the tears. Oh, what it means to look at the pictures and relive those moments again! It seems so real, and it was. I can almost reach out and touch him again and feel his hug, so big and surrounding. I can almost hear his voice, "Hey, Dad." Then I am driven to my knees to realize he is gone. My son is gone. But never take the pictures. Always leave me the pictures.

The Pictures
(August 10, 2002)

I have them everywhere,
the pictures of Joe,
the pictures in my mind.

When I look,
they tell me it is not true,
Joe is not gone,
I can see him,
the same in the pictures as before,
I can almost feel him as I did then,
I can recapture the moment.

He is not gone,
he is still here,
the pictures tell me so,
and speak to me of memories,
treasured times with Joe,
and as long as I can relive the feeling,
I will look and look
and look.

32.

I must find new meaning to my life. Everything I have done has been in a world which had Joe. Things made sense in such a world. Now, Joe is gone. That world is gone. Another has taken its place. I must redefine what has meaning now. I can do the things I did before, but they are not the same. My world is not the same. Yet, they are part of my connection to Joe, these things I did with him. I will keep them up, re-enacting parts of my life done with Joe, preserving the continuum between my life and his.

Continuum
(August 10, 2002)

There has been a break in time
and in me
with Joe's dying,
the world ahead so unknown,
signs of recognition seen,
but how can I trust them after this?
How I wish Time would stop,
keep me in this moment,
as, unrelenting, it takes me farther
from the time Joe was here.

But,
Joe was here,
he left a connection with me,
thirty one years of us to carry on,
every smile, every tear, his gentle touch,
and the hugs like no other,
he gave them all,
mementos of his being to help my way,
a continuum of time leading home,
leading back to Joe to stay.

33.

I find that part of me is afraid to hope. So many of my hopes were lost when Joe died. I find myself bracing for what may come next. The world seems so bleak, a more fearful and foreboding place. Why hope, I wonder, why dream, if it can all be ended in an instant? The injustice of it all! They say that Time heals. How can I trust Time if what awaits is something like this? What choice do I have? I cannot live expecting only the worst. I must hope and pray for the best and for the strength to endure what comes. Is this not God's promise? He will provide the strength to endure. Endure I must if I can.

Afraid
(August 10, 2002)

Hope died, too, that day
with Joe,
and fear crept in.
What next?
What dreams have yet to end?
Where do I go from here?

The world is so more menacing,
it can happen to me,
to my family again,
my guard now always up,
unsettled by what I cannot see,
waiting, watching,
like a silent sentinel,
not knowing the enemy,
only that the enemy will come.

When will it be safe to hope again?
I cannot man the watch forever,
my guard will be let down,
and then, will it happen again?

34.

It is my birthday. August 11. A time to celebrate as we did on all such occasions. A family dinner for birthdays and special events—a job change, a move, a graduation, an award—always at a fine restaurant. We had our favorites. This was Joe's. But this time, he was not here. Should we go? It would be painful and incomplete, hard to celebrate at all, much less there. The more I thought, the more I was convinced we had to go. We should not avoid places Joe loved which held such memories. How could we not do what we would have done with Joe, what he would have wanted to do? Worse, how could we go anywhere else? We would be haunted by the memories of what we were trying to avoid and would not even feel them in the familiar surroundings where Joe would want to be. It would be so much harder, and I would feel guilty for it. No, I decided, we had to go. We would cry at Joe's absence, but our very tears would bring us closer to him and make him part of the occasion as he always was. I will include him always. I will shrink from no memory, no matter how great the pain to feel it. Feel it I will. I will feel for Joe forever.

Celebration
(August 10, 2002)

It has come round again,
as I knew it would,
the first celebration without Joe,
my birthday as it happened to be,
what struggle what to do.

Dinner at the usual place?
It was Joe's favorite,
or shun the occasion and pretend?
Pretend what?
That Joe would not be
wherever we would be?
We could not hide.
Would his absence be more bearable alone?
Would the pain and tears be less at home?

OH JOE!

In the end we went,
the decision mine,
facing the pain I knew would come,
but at least a pain I knew,
only made worse,
I feared,
to avoid a place and time Joe loved,
and I, convinced that on that night,
at that place,
Joe would be there,
as he always was,
not sitting at home,
but there where he would want to be.

35.

Once again, sometimes it seems Joe is not gone. He is just not here right now, like other times when he was at work, or at home, or out of town, or when we did not talk for awhile. He would call later. I remember that feeling. I have the same feeling now. It is so familiar. How I want to believe it is true. Maybe it is. Maybe he will call. Joe, please call.

Not Gone
(August 13, 2002)

Sometimes, it seems,
you are not gone,
just gone away for awhile,
just out of sight for now,
a phone call away,
you will be off work soon,
we'll visit then, at your house or mine,
sometimes I pretend.

But as time goes on,
it is too long,
and I know,
from the aching deep within,
I know,
the phone will not ring,
you will not call,
you are not coming back,
and I cry for the pretense.

I would accept the delusion gladly
if it would stay,
give me even one more day,
but I know you left yourself with us,
thirty one years of you,
enough to carry me for the rest

of what is left for me to do,
a lifetime to visit and recall,
your lifetime with me through it all.

No, you are not gone,
just not here right now,
out of sight until we see each other again,
when, my time up, I reach my end.

36.

The world has changed. Without Joe, things are not the same. I awake each morning, and it hits me. It is my first thought. I wake into this unknown land where nothing is certain, where time, so long seemed at my whim, can turn on you in a heartbeat. I find it hard to make sense of what I see. I look about, but what does it mean? It was part of a world I knew that is gone. It did not exist independently of Joe. He was as much a part of it as me. He helped define what it meant to me. What is its place for me now? What is mine? I can go through the motions of the things I did before, but they are more rote than ever. They mean less, perhaps nothing. How do I live in a world without Joe?

Changed
(August 13, 2002)

Sleep has abandoned me
to a world unknown, unseen before.
I cannot recall the world before you were here,
and now it returns, unbidden, unwanted.

All about they are there,
the sun, the sky, the trees,
the wind and sights and sounds of life,
the people, too, all now so alien,
and I no longer belonging.

I am in a dream, a trance,
on the outside looking in,
in this strange land, feeling my way,
searching for who I am,
remembering only who you and I used to be.

How I long for home, for you!
You took so much of me with you
I do not know what is left.

37.

Joe, I miss you, son. As I watched you leave, I screamed inside, "Take me with you. Don't leave me here." You are such a part of me. You are in the fabric of my life. I want to go with you, to watch over you, to protect you as I tried to do your whole life. Wherever you go, I should be with you. I am your Dad. I do not want to be left without you. I do not want that part of my life gone. Then, I realize, I am with you. Part of me left when you did. Part of me died when you died. And so much of you is left with me. Our time together cannot be taken back. It leaves me memories to recall and lessons learned to live. You have shaped me in countless ways and will live on with me through it. Thank you, son, for being you. You mean so much to me.

Take Me With You
(August 14, 2002)

When Joe died,
part of me cried inside,
"Take me with you".
I could not imagine
your leaving forever without me,
I did not want to stay in a world
so touched by you
and now without you,
I wanted to be there with you
as you passed into this void unknown,
with all its promises,
still unknown,
not wanting you to be alone.

"Take me with you,"
I cried inside,
let me be there for you
as I have always tried,

and know always that I am,
across every distance I must span.

So much of my life is in yours,
it cannot be taken out,
it follows wherever you go,
all I have given and taught,
how I have loved you so,
you take me with you,
as you leave yourself with me,
know always, son,
I am there by your side.

38.

I do not want to adjust to a world without Joe. I do not want to leave behind the world that had you in it. But I do not face such a world. I look about and see a world larger and better because you were here. You have left me a bettered world. I cannot disown it or retreat from it. It is your legacy to me. This world you touched will forever have your touch upon it. I must try, hard as it is, to embrace it, to recognize you in it, to savor your imprint upon it.

Adjusting
(August 24, 2002)

All I can think or feel
is the sorrow of a world
without Joe,
Adjust, you say?
There will be no adjusting
for I have no interest in a world
without Joe.

But I do not face such a world.
No!
I am left with the world as Joe
left it to us,
a world in which he had a place
and played a part,
and played it well and touched our hearts.
What a legacy it is!

This is the adjusting to be done,
to a world still with Joe, my son,
only his presence with us changed,
but a presence that nonetheless remains,

this, the world I now face,
a world by Joe forever graced,
a world he found so worth living,
still so alive with him,
still so alive for me,
Joe everywhere I see.

39.

The world has become for me more cold and foreboding without Joe. How could it happen? Where once was hope and joy and future plans, there are now new fears, more to dread, the haunting wait for what next. Am I left to steel myself for what comes, with no purpose but to deal with what is dealt to me, afraid to hope or plan, waiting for the phone to ring in the night when no one has reason to call? What of joy? I cannot imagine it now. I feel guilty at the thought, as if it would somehow betray you that I could feel happiness without you. Are we all expendable? Or do we have an unspoken pact to go on, not needing saying, implied in all that we do? I think it must be so or all we give to each other would be lost in mourning. Your life means more to me than that. You showed us how to live. Despite the odds, in the face of the burdens, you took Life on and loved it. If I have learned anything, it is that I must do the same. As hard as it is, I must. As hard as it was for you, you did.

The Pact
(August 30, 2002)

The world is desolate now
that Joe has died.
Maybe, somewhere out there,
there is happiness and joy to be found,
though I cannot see it or sense it from here,
but more, is it for me?
Joy or laughter that signals something
good and right when all is so wrong?

How do I feel emotions shared with Joe
when Joe is not here?
Is it selfish and betrayal,
as if,
if I can feel them alone,
feeling it with Joe was less,
that Joe was less a part of it?

No!
What I felt with Joe can never
be diminished,
it was then, now is now,
my joy with Joe proof
such joy can be had,
and had once more,
Joe would have it no other way,
no misplaced honoring,
no dungeoning of mirth,
everything we felt together
feeling again.

Have we a pact with Life and each other
to live despite despair,
the pain and the sorrow,
owing to each other to go on
if we can?
Are we bound this way
to Life and to live,
if you cannot, must I go on for you?

Is there a pact that we will carry on
and meet again when we are gone,
the meeting place agreed,
the date and time yet decreed?
You, now waiting,
cheer me on,
as you did when you were here,
as you do still, still so near.

40.

Part of me died with you, Joe. You did not leave alone. Part of me went with you. I can feel its going, the emptiness that once was you and me. It will be no more. But it has gone somewhere. It did not cease to exist. Once created between us, it is there for all time. It cannot be undone. For thirty-one years, it was here. Now it is with you. I hope it comforts you, that you can feel my presence and know I am with you still. This part of you is left with me, too. I feel it every day. I cry for your going and sometimes laugh as I relive the times we laughed. I do the things we used to do, for you are there. I feel you in so many places if I look, but it is so hard to look. The crying comes easier.

My Death, Too
(August 30, 2002)

I died, too, that day
when Joe left.

As I hugged him that last time,
part of me did not let go,
I did not loosen my embrace
all the way,
less of me backed away,
no longer whole,
enough of me to see,
but the rest laid down with Joe,
gone with him,
he is not alone,
father and guardian,
I am there.

Part of Joe did not die that day,
the part that did not go,
the pictures he gave us of his life,
his sayings and his doings,
his deep felt feelings,

OH JOE!

how much he loved,
all I learned,
remembrances without end.

Part of Joe did not let go that day,
he holds me still,
and always will.

41.

I sometimes think I no longer know how to pray. I prayed so hard for Joe to recover, the prayers, the rosaries, the masses, the visits to the chapel in the hospital. Still he died. In my head, I know that God answers all prayers in His own way, though we may not see it at the time. I want to believe that, somehow unknown to me, my prayers were answered here, but I cannot see it. I wonder, if that is true, if whatever happens is God's answer to our prayer, why pray for a result? Why should not the prayer simply be, "God, do whatever you're going to do because you're going to do it anyway"? What of requests that are granted? Why some and not others? Why did God not save Joe? He could have but chose not to. Why? In the midst of these thoughts, when I was feeling most rejected and abandoned by God, I read something from the Bible—nothing new, I had read it many times before—and had an insight not had before. I read again about Christ praying in the Garden of Gethsemane the night before his crucifixion. He prayed to his Father: "*Abba* (O Father), you have the power to do all things. Take this cup away from me. But let it be as you would have it, not as I." (Mark 14: 36). Three times he pleaded with the Father to avoid his impending death. Still He died. God chose not to answer the prayer of His only Son. In not answering my prayers to save Joe, I thought, God did not treat me any differently than His own Son. Not that this makes Joe's death easier to bear, but I am less blaming of God. I do not feel as abandoned and alone. I will pray again and hope. There is no other way.

Prayer
(August 30, 2002)

How am I to pray?
I used to know,
then,
when I had hopes of answer,
when there was a God that listened
as He said He would.

And so I asked,
as hard as I could,
and waited, forever it seemed,

my hopes dragged along
with Time as it passed,
dimming with each days dying light,
as death came nearer,
as my prayers became louder,
as I pleaded in all the words I knew,
and then Joe was gone.

Have I been betrayed,
mere holder of fools gold as I prayed?
Or was I heard,
in ways I cannot see,
for reasons unknown to me,
some truth out there to be found,
but found or not,
that keeps me bound,
bound to hope and prayer again,
and that we are bound all
to God's end.

42.

I have appreciated the condolences and expressions of concern from friends and business acquaintances. On a business call one day, I was asked more than usual how I was doing. I was grateful to talk of it. I appreciated most the call back. This friend called just to say that if I needed to talk, he was there. You do not know how much that meant. I thanked him and hung up. Then I called back to let him know he had made a difference. So many times we make a difference and never know it. I wanted him to know.

The Call Back
(September 14, 2002)

I did not wait for the phone to ring,
I had given up long ago,
there was no time,
or so I had to believe,
what else could it be?

And then, the ringing,
the call back,
no reason, not expected, not required,
and still it came,
as if meant just for me,
a friend,
business talk over, condolences done,
this was something else.

Could it be me?
There were so few,
how could I know?
But I did, I knew,
and the day was at once more bearable
knowing this concern for me.

43.

There was a sermon at Mass that struck me. Again, it was nothing new, nothing I had not thought of before. This time it was said in a way that made me think of Joe and how I am struggling to make sense of this new world that confronts me. The priest reminded us that nothing remains the same and explained that this is not the point. We are constantly being remade as we are forced to adapt to the changes around us. The question is, "Where is God leading us?" For all the seeming randomness, out of this wilderness God is leading us somewhere, to be something more, to do something different. All is not pointless. There may not be a purpose to what happens or when, but there is a purpose to what we are to do with it and where we are to go from there. I have no answers. All I can do is to be open to what God may want of me from this.

The Remaking
(September 18, 2002)

I know nothing of this remaking
of me since Joe died,
remade before in so many subtle ways,
what is happening now?
Whose hand is behind this undoing,
How does he shape me?
What am I to do but wait?
Out of my hands long ago,
try as I might,
it seems I count for nothing.
I am being remade for something,
but what?

44.

Joe's death was hard enough when it happened. Since then, I lose him again each day. I relive his going each time I wake and must begin again to face a world without Joe. Each day I lose him more as Time takes him farther from me, as life without him goes on and accumulates in my mind and memory, displacing the past as it goes, not for good, but pressing it into deeper recesses. I mourn this movement away, this slow going, this loosening hold on my consciousness. I want it to stop, this fading of the past. It is a new loss every day, and my sadness grows.

Losing You
(October 5, 2002)

Joe,
each day I lose you
all over again,
as Time does its work,
forcing more and more into history,
each day taking you farther from me,
from my last sight and feel of you
that must last me a lifetime.

No wonder I fight Time so,
the fading and the shading,
as my fears grow,
what details will be lost
in each remembering,
fine points here and there,
the edges rounded,
the surface smoothed,
it adds up.

When does it become just a memory?
How do I remember well enough
as the minutes and hours of my days

are stolen from me,
only to find when I turn my attention
to you,
you are farther away,
each day more of you lost,
each day less of you to lose.

How can I make it stop?
How can I make you stay?

45.

It comes in waves. One moment, I think I am doing better; the next, I am overcome with sadness and grief and the realization that Joe is gone. How helpless and hopeless I feel! It may be triggered by a familiar sight or sound, a place or circumstance shared with Joe never to be shared again, or it may be nothing in particular at all. At times, I am adrift with no land in sight. For all my efforts to compensate, my attempts to regroup, Joe is gone. Nothing can change this.

Waves
(October 19, 2002)

It comes in waves,
the grief and pain ever so present
suddenly overwhelms,
and all else fades to nothingness,
there is only me and Joe,
our family,
and that is all I want to be,
again.

Emotions, checked for a time
but never for long,
soon crest again
by my remembering,
there is so much to feel,
I do not want to stop,
for Joe is there,
I can feel him.

And then I feel the swell subsiding,
the tears drying,
as if Joe is moving from me,
and the emptiness returns,
until the next wave
brings Joe to me again.

46.

I experience everything less now except pain. I go through the motions, but I cannot summon much to put into them. I am going on memory, things familiar enough to know what to do until I can retreat into myself away from demands that seem so trivial. They are draining me. How can they mean anything to me when I have lost my son?

How Do I Fit?
(October 21, 2002)

There is a world going on
about me,
but I am not in it,
I have not left the world just gone,
the world with Joe.
What am I doing here?
What am I to do?

I can recall forces of habit,
places I must be,
but I view them from afar,
spying upon a hostile world
searching for signs of recognition,
in a time warp.

My mind, my heart lags what I see,
it is so distant,
what does it have to do with me?
How do I fit here,
not wanting to leave where I am
as the world goes on
and takes me with it?

I will fit
because Joe is here,
he left his mark upon the world
and us,
and we, forever marked with him,
do not survive alone,
but it is so hard.

47.

It is the early morning hours again. I am overcome with feelings vying for my attention, demanding my time, struggling to co-exist. Reason tries to sort out emotion; rationalization attempts to make sense of what has happened; grief and sorrow demand to be felt; fears of the future make their case; and the clock relentlessly marches toward the days work. I do not know what will surface next. They must be put down as I embark on the day, not quieted for good, flaring up off and on, biding their time until they can get me in bed again. It is so tiring. I feel every emotion there is to feel, struggling to survive them, to make sense of what they mean. At times, I surrender, a break from the battle. It is then, when I stop, that I am overwhelmed by the devouring sense of sadness.

Maelstrom
(October 23, 2002)

What do I feel?
I scarcely know,
they come at me from all sides,
emotions and thoughts dragging me high and low,
buffeting me about,
roiling,
forcing tears back and forth
across hope and despair,
the line so thin,
so hard to know what side I'm in,
locked in a struggle,
my head desperately trying to sort
the woundings and grievings of my heart,
tears and smiles of memory,
all changing one moment to the next,
and I, at their mercy,
doing my best,

not knowing what will come,
what it will mean or what will be done,
Time, perhaps, to have the final say,
or does that change, too, day to day?

48.

Mark and I have spoken often about Joe's death. Mark was so close to his brother. He and Joe talked about everything, and he says there is so much more he wanted to talk with Joe about. Things come up now he would have asked Joe. We both find ourselves asking, "What would Joe have done?" We valued his opinion. Not only because he is my son and for Mark, his brother. It was how he lived his life. Joe did things his way, on his terms, without putting up a front. His attitude was, "This is who I am." He did not try to package himself to please others. Those who knew Joe accepted him. You need only look at the cards, the flowers, the website condolences, the words written in the book, to see how widely Joe was loved. We still find what Joe would have done to be a good measure of how we are looking at a problem. We still want his input, and we are able to have it from the example of his life.

What Would Joe Have Done?
(October 24, 2002)

How often we ask,
what would Joe have done?
What would he say?
I sometimes think
we never asked enough,
there was always time,
another time,
next time,
and now the time is here
and Joe is gone.

But we asked enough to know,
enough to ask again,
Joe left us with this,
what he felt and thought,
the thoughts and musings of his heart.
He told so many that miss his words,
who now ask again to be heard,

what would Joe say or do,
knowing enough
to know what he would say,
what he would do,
asking again just to know it's true.

49.

It was on the drive to work one morning. The day started like all the rest. I cannot believe what has happened. I choke and I cry. Then, "Push back," I thought. The only way to deal with Life's defeats, with its turns and its burdens, is to push back. Do not be timid or afraid. Do not surrender or give up. This is the only way to cope. Life deals most harshly with those who will not try. Take Life's dare. Meet it head on. Above all, go down trying. It will not happen on its own. It comes from within us. This is the one thing I wanted to impart to Joe and Mark: the ability to live fully in the world and to deal with what Life delivers. They learned well, and I am proud of them. Both are unafraid. Both made their way undaunted. How courageous Joe was in his life! How courageous Mark has been with Joe's passing! I must do the same. I must push back at Life. Not to taunt or dare, but we must not stay down. We must get up. We must go on. We must not allow Life to leave us this way.

Push Back
(October 30, 2002)

I am down, defeated,
Joe is gone.
Life, it seems, has won
despite all I have done.
It would be so easy to stop,
the slightest effort sometimes seems too much,
what chance have I against
the approaching unknowns,
have I only terms of surrender?

No!
I must push back, push back at Life,
from my knees, on my back,
I must push back,
go forth into the breach,

for there is no escaping Life's deadly reach,
make Life face me,
do not be taken without a fight,
strike back undaunted by Life's seeming might,
this engaging and contending my only chance
to be counted in Life's diddling dance,
to grab Life's attention and earn its respect,
to have any hope of having an effect.

It is not just on your terms, Life,
I have something to say,
it is my terms, too,
you will face each day,
no easy way with me, Life,
for I will push, too,
and for all your resisting
some pushes will get through.

I will not be taken without a word,
for I have much to say
and much to be heard,
and all my sayings and all I do
will all become a part of you,
but if I do not push back
you will never know
what I had to say and had to show.

And so as part of Life I must play the part,
and not default to what Life has wrought,
and, once added to the fray,
I must push back to seize another day,
a day of mine with hopes and dreams
not yet ended by Life as it seems.

OH JOE!

You may have me yet, Life,
and will claim me in time,
but for the time I have left, Life,
I will have it as mine.

50.

Sooner or later, something must be said about the platitudes. Everything works out for the best. Our prayers were answered. God knows best. For reasons we may not be able to see, and hard as it may be to understand, this was best for Joe. There is a purpose to what happens. Time heals all. Give it a year. We should count our blessings. The words seem so trite, so demeaning to me and my loss. They diminish what I feel. They do not understand. But platitudes became platitudes for a reason. They express a truth about the human condition, observed and proved over time. They are recurring statements about existence, predictors of how things will be, not all the time, not without exception, but enough times for enough people to offer hope that the same may be true for me. Will I be an exception?

Platitudes
(October 30, 2002)

Platitudes,
how often have I heard you,
how often dismissed you as not my concern?
Until I find myself within your reach,
what have you to do with me?
You cannot know what I have suffered,
it is not as simple as you say.

Yes,
I yearn for solace.
Yes,
I long for comfort,
but aimed for me,
not dispensed for some other tragedy.
Try not to justify what has happened,
nor explain it away,
there is no sense to be made of this,
nothing you can say.

But, you say,
it is not sense you offer,
only the promise I can survive,
as others like me have done
and remained alive,
alive and one day ready to live again,
enough for you to say
I can live until then,
so much more of Life to be lived
and for me to do,
and you leave me
with these words spoken to:

Do not expect more from Life than
Life is meant to give,
or think it is other than it is,
it has a place for now,
but it is not the end,
only the bridge to reunion again.

51.

I try to put Joe's passing into some kind of perspective. I focus so much on my loss, the outcome I wanted, insisting that my prayers be answered the way I asked because this is what I feel. What was best for Joe? All I have ever wanted was the best for him. Is that what this was? I do not want to feel only bitterness because I no longer have Joe. I must step outside myself and think of him. At least my grief may be tempered by the joy I know Joe now feels. I will see him again and will speak with him each day until I do. Ahead, there are so many of our family to greet him: my Mom and Dad; my brother; my grandparents; Peggy's Dad; uncles and aunts. Joe loved them all. They will care for him until I am there. And while I bide my time, I will strive to do my best here.

Outside Myself
(October 30, 2002)

I am consumed by Joe's dying
and what I have lost,
unable to follow
into where he has crossed,
but it does him no service
to dwell only on this,
it is his life to be honored
in all that we miss.

A lifetime with Joe
it flashes through my mind,
in leaps and bounds,
his spirit soaring and lifting me,
found in everywhere I see,
these are the memories to cherish and hold
until we are gathered again in the fold.

Until then let me not speak only
of my loss and my pain,
let the talk be of Joe

OH JOE!

and his mark that remains,
this gift of his life he gave to us,
let us live it well and live it in trust.

52.

More than anything, I am diminished. There is less of me now. Part of me is no longer here. Everything seems less, less point to what I do, less behind my efforts. The motions are merely gone through. They are more forced, but at least they are forced and will be gone through the next day and the next.

Diminished
(October 30, 2002)

Joe is gone,
and, more than anything,
I am diminished.
There is less of me now than before,
a part of me left with him,
the part that was father and friend.

I go on with things left to be done,
now left to do without my son,
things no longer to be shared with Joe,
no stories to tell for him to know,
and they are the less,
not for those still in the telling and sharing,
but less for us without Joe and his caring.

I shout them out,
and whisper them through tears,
but only silence about,
no answers to hear,
and I am diminished,
kept inside, they are not enough untold
to fill the void or warm the cold,
and I am less.

53.

Time heals they say. But how? It has already taken so much. Will it now take what is left? This steady honing of the edges of memory and sharpness, a slow fading away. Is it not healing, but not remembering as much, less to hurt, and this loss, the worst of all? Robbed of Joe's life, will Time not be satisfied until it has taken his memory from me, too?

Times March
(November 8, 2002)

Time marches on
with a mind of its own,
a swagger as if it owned the world,
setting the pace
to do with me what it will,
exacting, extracting how much
until the price is paid.

How much to satisfy this appetite?
Insatiable, relentless,
clearing memories as it goes,
new happenings pushing to the front,
no reverence for the past,
condemned to be forgotten,
if Time has its way,
too soon for the future not yet allowed,
only Time will tell.

Who are you Time?
Goth-draped grim reaper
or white knight of hope?

OH JOE!

For all our planning,
we are only what you allow,
the only time, now,
until time runs out.

54.

People go on as if things are the same. They may be for them, but not for me. What do they expect of me? To go on as if nothing has changed? Everyone is willing to allow some time—some more, some less—but then, they say, I must get over it. I must get on with life. But I am not the same. I will never be the same again. How do I fit in a world that is the same for everyone but me? When am I supposed to rejoin a world gone awry and forever changed? After what period of time? After what cathartic experience? After what?

When
(November 14, 2002)

I must get over it,
it is easy for you to say
from the outside looking in,
but when?

When would you have me
put this behind?
Is there an appointed hour?
Do you fancy it is up to you
not me?
And how do I go about the doing?

You have little to say for
you do not leave this much behind,
much perhaps,
but not this,
the farewells are not so ready,
they may never be said.

OH JOE!

Time cannot undo what Time has wrought,
and so I feel my way in the dark,
wondering if the pain will end,
not knowing if Time will be
foe or friend.

55.

Tears are not enough to vent the pain, but they are all I have. Sometimes, the world seems to stop, and they flow. Other times, in the midst of the goings on, they force their way through, then the only thing that is real. This is Joe's way of speaking to me. It is the language of grief. It affirms Joe's continued presence, the realness of his life, how he still touches me and, through the tears, comforts me.

Tears
(November 18, 2002)

I speak now a language of tears,
this, the only way to express what I feel
at Joe's dying.

They speak up at any time
when they have something to say,
saying more than words can ever know,
they are how I speak to Joe,
and how he speaks to me,
telling me he is thinking of me,
his way of touching me
to assure me he is here,
his way of reaching me
to ease my pain through the tears,
his way of comforting me
in my fears.

And my tears speak to him
of love and longing and loneliness,
of thanks and hope and promises,
and of the day we will be together,
all of us again,
as we were then.

56.

We yearn for something constant, a way to be safe and secure. How are we to do this in a world constantly changing about us, a world in flux? There is no way to relax, to sit back without guard, for nothing stays the same. We are ever adjusting, responding, coping. The only constants are abstract ones, principles that have withstood the erosion and ravages of Time. They have survived. They are there to hold onto, transcending change, not dependent on it or us. Goodness, truth, honor, duty, love. These are what must guide us. They do not change. Lesser things—fear, cruelty, self-centeredness, unkindness—they are the works of our hands and depend upon us to give them life. They do not exist except as individual acts. They do not test Time because they can be undone by not doing. Not so with these other truths. They exist as ideals, immutable, unchanging, waiting to be embraced. It is these constants I must turn to if I am to survive.

The Constants
(November 23, 2002)

It is the constants
that will carry me through,
reminding me of reason to live
when Joe has been taken from me.

Happenings like this so tempt
abandoning of hope,
the allure of despair,
but there are larger truths afoot,
extending a hand to a world of change
and tragedy,
where nothing can be counted before its time.

They put the happenings in their place,
let them exact their grief, inflict their pain,
the grip will loosen over time,
never letting go,
but I can live with that,

these larger truths, these constants,
assure me that I can and why.

57.

Faced with a world that changes around us, sometimes unannounced, other times with deadly precision, what are we to make of now? Is the here and now all that is real, replacing what was and forever preceding what will be? How can we trust now when it will not stay? What place is there for plans that may never be? But there is a place because they may. There is no certainty they will be denied. They hold all the promises of now and must be given a chance.

Here and Now
(November 23, 2002).

How I miss the here and now
when you were here,
the plans, the hopes, the dreams,
now come to naught,
or have they?

They served their purpose at the time,
with a future fast approaching,
we could not wait,
and so we hoped, and planned and dreamed,
all part of the draught of life,
all part of the here and now, then.

I do not believe we looked too far ahead,
the looking was the joy,
the dreaming the spirit soaring,
the planning so much we shared,
how they enriched the here and now, then.

And now we face a future denied,
the only one we could see,
Joe's going, in truth, a step closer
to the future that will be.

58.

I was driving home from work listening to Pavarotti's Christmas CD. It was comforting, these religious songs in Latin—*Panis Angelicus, Ave Maria, Adeste Fidelis.* What is so soothing? What is their spell? It is, I think, their rich history, their roots in simpler times when belief was easier, less was questioned. Things seemed more certain. They were less doubted. They are part of a belief that has sustained others for two thousand years and, perhaps, can sustain me now. There is comfort in that which I need if only for the brief interlude of a song. In their way, they ease the pain and help me to believe there is a larger truth at work. If they have been so treasured throughout the ages, there must be something to treasure. They are a promise of hope I must have. Otherwise, what is the point? Doing for its own sake seems worth little. They are a bridge between the here and now and whatever else there is, not just the promise of continuing life for Joe, but a way for me to survive his leaving and the fear of my own going. They sing of the promise of more and that Joe is there and I will join him one day. It is something I must believe. But why this belief? Why not another? Perhaps it is conditioning or early teaching. These beliefs, all so competing, share something in common: a guarded hope that something more awaits us. It did not end with Joe. What is it? I cannot know for sure, but I believe Joe is there and I will follow. This consoles me.

The Bridge
(November 26, 2002)

Joe,
what stands between you and me?
The gulf seems so wide.
I look for you but cannot see
except the visions of you in my mind,
I listen for your voice but cannot hear
except the sounds of your words in my ears,
I reach for you but cannot touch,
and hold myself tight to imagine your hug.

Yet I know you are there,
this belief,

my only way to reach you now,
holding me up while I wait,
carrying my thoughts to you,
returning your prayers for me,
I can feel them,
they give me hope,
they give me promise,
this bridge to you,
one day to take me, too.

59.

On this same drive home from work, I thought of how others shy away from speaking of Joe, afraid to mention his name as if this will remind us that he has died and cause us pain. Do you think not saying the words will spare us a reminder of Joe? Do you not know that we think of Joe all the time? He is always in our thoughts. Not a day goes by that I do not grieve his passing. We do not forget. We want to remember. We have a need to talk of Joe and for you to speak of him, too. Reminisce with us and relive our shared memories. If we cry, these are not tears that would have gone unshed. We cry inside and out all the time. So let us talk of Joe often, with love and affection, and glorious times past. Share them with us.

Talk About
(November 26, 2002)

So many times
I wait for you to speak of Joe,
some word, some question,
some mention of his name.
What is it you fear?

As sorrowful as you feel for me,
as fearful for you as you may be,
the silence is far worse,
unsaid is not undone,
it is so real,
we must hear it from you
to help us through.

Do not leave us to go on alone
in a world that cannot speak of Joe as gone,
he was here and touched us each,
and is with us still within our reach,
if you will but say his name
and talk of him just the same.

OH JOE!

Let there be no worry
your words will slow our healing,
or resurrect our painful feelings,
the grief is here and here to stay,
restless beneath all we say,
needing sometimes but a word or so
to quench our need to talk of Joe.

60.

The Holidays are here. I could feel them coming as I sank lower into gloom. Dreaded, they rushed faster and faster toward me. Now they have arrived bringing every memory of Joe like it was yesterday, flailing me with every hope lost with Joe, every memory we will never know.

The Holidays
(December 21, 2002)

They were coming,
the holidays,
not feared at first when still far away,
and then, with their arrival, showing why
a reputation well earned,
their threat delivered at last,
sometimes, I think, the final blow,
the pictures in my mind more vivid
than a camera's eye,
portals to my heart.

These are the holidays,
crowding out all else,
no everyday demands to distract,
all else put aside,
there is nothing but this,
Joe is gone,
but the feeling still there
like a limb taken off,
a part of me never lost.

These holidays, they hit me
with a vengeance,
as I cry out for Joe,
and then just cry.

61.

Joe's death still seems so unreal. I know that despite all my holding on, more and more will take its place in memory, always there, but not as close to the surface. I fight it and resent it and rage against it. Will Time not leave well enough alone? Does Time never have enough? I do not want an instant of Joe to be displaced or relegated to what was. His presence in my life continues. His life in me lives on. How I hate Time for what it does, its lessening of the pain. This is all I have left of Joe. If that goes, will he go with it farther from me? How can I hold on? Must I let go to survive? Is it not Time but Joe that lessens his hold on me, not letting me go, but pushing me to go on? Despite all my wondering, all I can say is, "Joe, please don't leave me."

Holding On
(December 27, 2002)

I sit with the memories of Joe,
what else do I have,
as Time demands them, too,
taking them as it moves on,
and I rage and resist,
Time, have you not had enough,
would you have this, too?

So I hold on
to the loss, to the pain,
to my memories of Joe,
holding on for dear life,
fighting Time and all its dimming,
as slowly Time collects its winnings.

Or is it Joe
that lessens his hold on me,
bidding me to go on,
his blessing as I go,
his steady hand at my side,

his hugging arms opened wide,
his place in my heart forever fixed
to help me survive even this.

62.

The Christmas holidays were bearing down upon us. What about a trip? Maybe it would help to get away. Not to forget, but to remove the familiar, since during this time the familiar is empty and incomplete without Joe. Would it be easier to think of him and remember him somewhere else? Life for us is different now. Should we do something different? And so we did. London on New Year's Eve. Then Paris. It snowed. Then we came home, and I cried that Joe was not here.

The Trip
(December 28, 2002)

How far did we travel,
and why?
Not far enough,
where is there to go?
Would we if we could?

I cannot leave,
it is hard enough for a time,
never forever,
I will not let go,
holding fast to the memories
and the history,
holding on for dear life,
for how dear is life,
never so close,
never so far away,
now that Joe is gone
and I am here.

I will be there, son,
someday,
I know not when,
the same hand as yours
yet to write my end.

63.

It was on the trip, seeing the sights, an ancient church in Bath. I entered a chapel for private prayer. I sat and thought of Joe and us. I looked about, and everywhere I saw signs of Joe. I prayed.

Everywhere
(December 29, 2002)

I see Joe everywhere,
a sight, a sound seen before with him,
a sight, a sound he would have liked,
something he would have said,
a wondering what he would say,
places gone together,
places left to go with him.

All the plans, all the dreams,
and then time ran out,
taking him with it,
leaving regrets at every turn,
but we could not know,
or live as if there were no tomorrow
with Joe,
nor did he,
as he charged into life headlong,
headstrong.

How I treasure these memories
of Joe,
and suffer for the memories
not to come,
the pain the worse because
I can see them,
and feel them,

OH JOE!

but I give thanks,
thanks that I see Joe everywhere
still here with me,
as I know he always will be.

64.

Everything is a struggle now. It takes more work. It saps my strength. The same interest is not there. There is less meaning. I worked for life to be a certain way and it was. There was context to what I did, and Joe was a part. He was such a part of me until now. What is the point if my efforts can be undone in the blink of an eye? What is the point if I cannot change what has happened?

Effort
(January 6, 2003)

Everything takes more effort now,
it is heavier, more dense,
gravity is stronger,
more resistance to overcome,
it is so wearying,
the familiar makes it easier,
but not caring drains that, too.

I go through the motions weighed down,
force of habit all I can muster,
my doings only because I must,
no interest unless forced,
my heart is not in it,
empty gestures, expected words,
I am an actor on a stage.

What is the point?
It is all so fleeting,
Joe,
one moment here,
one moment not,
but he was here
with me for a time,
and left behind a lifetime of signs.

OH JOE!

This I will have as on I go
into the world bequeathed by Joe,
struggling until I see him again,
loving him all the while til then,
left with my tears and fears,
and yes, laughter at times,
laughter that comes so hard,
maybe this, a gift, too,
your way of staying with us, Joe,
until we come to you.

65.

It was in a movie. The line was said, "It's not supposed to be this way." I thought of these words by the priest at Joe's funeral service. It was so true. In the movie, though, the response was, "Maybe it is." I wondered, is that it? Does the fact that something happens mean it was supposed to be that way? All the prayers, all the efforts of so many, and still Joe died. Was it supposed to be that way? When we say, "No," is this only from our perspective? It is what we want. Is it true only from the usual way life unfolds, not a fixed rule as to how it will? Is it meant to be that way as part of God's plan? Or because Life is random and follows no rules? Is nothing supposed to be any way? Can we count on anything? Can we do no more than react to what occurs? I wonder still.

This Way
(January 11, 2003)

How was it supposed to be?
Surely not this way,
not Joe's time now.

True,
the usual rules did not apply,
disease making its claim,
but Joe keeping it at bay,
taming its threats,
he was ahead,
slowing time to make it last,
making us believe,
and we did,
as he believed, too.

And then,
with a suddenness so violent,
it returned,
asserting its claim,
demanding Joe now.

OH JOE!

Was it meant to be this way?
Could Joe cheat its taking only so long?
Was it now? Was it wrong?
How can I know?
Only God can tell
and He has not told.

66.

I go by the cemetery sometimes before work. It is on the way. This is one of the reasons we chose this place. It keeps Joe close to us. I need these visits, these moments alone at the grave, moments alone with Joe. Sometimes I have no interest in going on with the day if I do not visit here. It is there, alone, that I pour out the grief welled up within me, a release of my heart. I feel better because I am able to share this with Joe. Son, I will be back soon.

Moments Alone
(January 12, 2003)

I go often to the grave,
as Life picks up its pace,
needing these moments alone with Joe,
for I am out of step with Life
since his going.
I need this closeness to where he lies
to right myself,
readied for the coming day,
a day seeming so much without meaning,
what I will do pales before what has been done.

So many tears left to shed,
so many shed here,
there is no better place,
this, my new language with Joe,
the only way I know to embrace him
and hold him close,
never again to feel his hug,
at least I have this,
these moments alone with Joe,
waiting, waiting until I see him again.

67.

There is something about my visits to the grave. There is such peace there. The rest of the world goes on, but it is stopped here. My heart quickens as I approach, and then, the stone in sight, they come, the tears. Held back so often, they are released here. They could flow, I sometimes think, without end, ending only when I walk away, even then, not all at once, only slowing to a stop for now, never for good.

At the Grave
(January 18, 2003)

The world has stopped,
I am frozen in time,
on the day Joe died,
on the day he was laid to rest.

Joe and the world have gone on,
but not me,
I am still at the grave,
waiting,
unable to say good-bye,
feeling Joe's presence
on Joe's ground,
knowing he is there,
for all the talk of where he may go,
where he may be,
I know he is here,
where I can find him.

Someone like me left the ground
that day,
on to home, on to work,
even play,
but not me,
I am standing here still

OH JOE!

at the grave,
alone,
weeping.

68.

Mark told us of a dream. Although it was his, it needs telling here. How happy I am for Mark! I wish I had been there. I want this dream, too. I can't wait to dream again.

The Dream
(January 18, 2003)

Sleeping,
suddenly, I heard a voice,
a voice I know so well,
"Hey, Mark."
I turned and it was Joe,
he looked the same,
he looked at me,
and reached,
arms wrapping large around me,
missing me as I miss him.

How I know that hug!
It was Joe, I could feel him,
I hugged back,
as hard as I could,
holding on, wanting it to last,
and I cried.

Then, it seemed, I woke,
or was it waking?
I was crying as before,
and aching,
reaching, reaching to where
Joe should be,
crying out,
"Joe, come back, come back to me!"

OH JOE!

Wondering through the tears,
was it a dream?
Was he really here?

69.

Mark asked me if I talk to Joe out loud at the grave. He had just been there. He knows I go there often. "Yes," I said, "I do." I thought of why. Silent thinking, muted prayer, many times is not enough. It has a place, but it has its limits. Somehow, saying the words out loud makes them more real, as if I am talking to Joe. I like to speak to him as if he is still here. Somehow, through the talking, it seems he is.

Out Loud
(January 20, 2003)

I stand there,
my eyes fixed upon the stone,
thoughts forming, tears welling,
tears falling,
as I fall, too,
deeper, faster.

So much runs through my head,
so much unsaid,
turning over and over
in silent communion with Joe,
but wanting more,
yearning for a voice
to bring him closer,
to make him real.

And so I speak out loud,
telling him how I miss him
and of my love,
and of my day ahead
and what I ask of him,
and the saying helps
to keep Joe with me,
no longer reduced to thought,

OH JOE!

less gone than before
if he is there to talk to,
bringing him back to earth.

70.

Time has gone on and so have I. One day unfolds into the next. They run together. So much to do. So much put off because I had to. I turn my attention to it again, but it is different now. Nothing is the same. I go through the same paces, do what I did before, but it is not the same. There is less invested in what I do. It is hollow. I wonder "why" more. What does it mean? More this, more that, but less of what matters. What matters now? There is much, but not as much. I pick up the pieces each day and try. Will it ever matter as much again?

Flashbacks
(January 22, 2003)

Another day dawns,
its coming known,
and I, prepared, throw myself in,
what is the choice?

And so I try and do,
and do well,
sometimes I think I am winning,
and then they come,
the flashbacks,
Joe here, Joe there,
Joe is everywhere,
every memory at once,
especially the best,
and they were so good,
I never knew how much,
my son, my life.

I welcome them,
these flashbacks,
full of loss as they are,
they are in me,
and I need their return to prove my life,

OH JOE!

as on I go trying and doing,
but for all my doing,
all my winnings,
I am still so sad.

71.

It is lonely behind the façade. Armed with it most days, I go forth to meet the world with the face they expect. It is all they know. The demands that await call for more than my grief displayed. They have no time. I must make the time for me with those who will have me. In between, I continue the façade. Sometimes, it takes so much.

The Façade
(January 26, 2003)

I am in hiding again,
in refuge behind the façade,
the tortured smiles,
the trappings of the game,
standing guard over the wounded child
for whom nothing is the same.

But my emotions are not held tightly enough,
some cascade through
until they have expressed enough to survive,
or I back them down until my time,
the mask of normalcy resumed,
and everyone is happy.

Life is on the move
and sweeps me with it,
not yet ready to go,
and so I put on this face you see,
this mask that has so little
to do with me.

72.

I think often about the face I put on each day. A look for the everyday of life. Why do I do it? Perhaps I owe it to others. I cannot expect them to feel what I feel or dwell on my sufferings with me. Time goes on and so do they, and I must give the appearance of going with them. Understanding and empathy have limits, I know. I am thankful for their concern, and, in return, I dress for them.

Dressing Up
(January 29, 2003)

Time to dress for another day.
What shall I put on?
What face to say I am fine?
What expression to say I am
going on?
What dabs of color
to hide the ashen look of pain?
What goals to achieve
to prove I am alive and well?
What form do I assume
to join the ranks of the living,
allowing me to pass for one of them?

They move on,
and so, I must have it seem to them,
do I,
and so I dress up,
it is easier this way
for Time weans the deepest sympathy,
there is no more time for this,
there are other callings.

What new barricades must guard
a heart and soul in flight,
fleeing on, no land in sight?

OH JOE!

What more for me to hide
while behind the mask
I die inside?

73.

Joe's birthday is approaching. What are we to do? Celebrate as usual in his honor? Or not leave the house and stay at home in mourning? How can we say now? We can only wait and see.

The Birthday Approaches
(February 2, 2002)

Joe's birthday,
it is coming as I knew it would,
once so far ahead,
it rushes to the front,
and I wait,
not in fearing,
not in wanting,
no wish to avoid or delay,
but in wondering.

The emotions are gathered there
for the feeling,
and I welcome them,
sent from Joe
to let me know he is with me,
his hand upon me to assure me
he is not gone,
his touch upon my heart
to say he cares.

He speaks to me in these memories,
these countless relivings
as we relive them again with him
in the grief and tears we share together
as we await his day.

74.

Some say, "You must get over it," the pain and the loss, "You must go on." There is truth to this, but, truth is, there is no way around it, no way to hasten it. The only path is through it, embracing it, feeling it, for as long as it takes. How long? A year? More? Less? Who are you to say? Who am I? It will be as long as it will be. What I need is that you be there for me, not to say, "Move on," but "Take your time, take as long as you need."

Through It
(February 3, 2003)

When did you become so expert
about my pain?
Telling me
I must get over it,
I must go on,
as if it could be put away like that,
as if it were all in my head
and could be decided away,
like making a will.
Would that it were,
then I could put up a fight
instead of this slow surrender,
but the pain holds all the cards.

No,
there is no turning away,
it is here to stay
and will have its way,
put down for a time,
but not put out,
coming and going as it will,
it owns me for now,
there is no way around,

only through,
feeling what must be felt,
or its presence will be made known
in other ways,
going by other names,
but always to be heard.

And so I will listen to the voice
for it has much to say,
and I will feel what must be felt
for that is pain's only way,
and mine, too,
to feel the pain and, feeling,
to feel my way through.

75.

Why is it so important to others that we say we are alright, that we are doing better? There is such discomfort if we are faring badly or poorly. The death of a child is every parent's worst fear. It could happen to you. If we can survive, it means you could, too. So you seek evidence that we can go on, desperate for proof that you could, too. If we do not do well, the loss may be even worse than you fear. The longer we do not do well, or at least say we are doing better, the worse the loss appears, the more afraid you may feel and choose to stay away. We are all pain averse.

Proof
(February 3, 2003)

You ask how I feel,
and I see it in your eyes,
concern, it is true,
but more,
fear this could be you.

What do you want of me?
I have so little to give,
for all your unspoken fears
of this happening to you,
mine are here
in this happening to me,
far worse than it seems,
much more than you can see,
for all your wishing me well
I wish, too,
that I survive this happening,
that it never happen to you.

But I can give you no proof,
no solace for your dread,
no words to comfort,

the words are not there to be had,
no pretended well being to ease your mind,
as I struggle for me in my own time.

I take it as it comes,
you must take me as I am,
with my hurting and my sorrow,
for each day, for each tomorrow,
until the day when I am ready to say
I am better again, better today.

76.

On a drive to work, I was once again struck by how much it seems Joe's dying is not real. I get up each day, come and go as before, things still have to be done. If I am doing them, how can it be true? I did these things when Joe was here. How can he not be now? When I close my eyes and try to imagine what has happened, I cannot believe it, though I know it is true. It is like it has happened in my mind and takes thinking even to conceive it. When I do, I am in mourning again as much as that first day.

Not Real
(February 5, 2002)

How can it be that Joe is gone
when my steady motions of habit carry on?
Duty calls,
the days take up my time,
the nights retreat,
I did all this before with Joe,
is he here in their doing
as I do them still?

How can it be true?
It takes all my imagining
to think the thought,
even then, like a dream,
and then my imaginings take hold,
and I am pierced through and through again,
staring in disbelief at the world going round me,
I, seeming to go with it,
but knowing better.

After all this time
I am in mourning again
as much as that first day,
frozen in Time,

OH JOE!

Time frozen in me,
wondering my place in a world
where this could be.

77.

On another drive to work, I tried to find words for what I was feeling, for the consuming sense of loss I still find so hard to believe. I am haunted by those days: the hospital, the funeral home, the arrangements, the service, the cemetery. Haunted that Joe is gone. What will I do?

The Haunting
(February 6, 2003)

I am haunted by them,
these images
of doctors and hospitals,
burial arrangers,
the crowd at the graveside,
leaving in their wake
loss and regret,
a cry for more time,
returning again and again
as if they had not had enough,
back to finish the job,
back to finish me off.

They imprint themselves,
these images,
seared into my mind,
indelible,
taking root, taking shape,
twisting and turning to stay alive,
rearing up if my thoughts begin to turn
lest their cut lessen.
Will the haunting never end?

78.

"I feel dull, blunted," Peggy said one night on the ride home after a movie. I realized that was it. The words described so well how we are since Joe died. We make the effort, but the attempts fall short. There is less put into it. There is less to put. Our spirits are closed off. Hopefully, one day the feelings will return.

Blunted
(February 7, 2003)

I know I must go on
but all in my head,
my heart lags behind,
still bound to the feelings of loss,
sunk in the emptiness,
such a struggle back up.

I try,
reaching out, reaching back,
longing for the touch,
only to find when it comes
I am still longing and waiting,
my senses dulled,
sensations blunted,
condemned to a lesser world
where I wander in search of Joe,
and wonder how far to go.

But I reach again,
hoping this time the feelings will return,
forcing as much as I can,
unable to force what is not there,
gathering my strength,
fending off until then,
in small steps feeling more,
as much as I dare,

OH JOE!

daring to feel
as much as I care.

79.

They say it takes a year to get over the death of a loved one. Why a year I have wondered? Why not more? Why not less? Is there something magical about a year? I heard one answer that may touch upon it: During the first year, we experience everything for the first time without Joe. Special days and occasions. Birthdays. His. Ours. Christmas. Easter. Family celebrations. There will only be this one first time. The first anniversary of each will only happen once. The loss will be there for all the years to come, but it will not be the first one. The rest will be different as the distance grows. Maybe that is it. I have yet to see.

First Year Coming
(February 13, 2003)

It is not a year yet
since Joe is gone,
as the year wears on and on,
special days come and go,
each the first without Joe,
each anniversary a new sorrow of its own,
cruel reminder of us alone,
and who has gone
and what has changed
in a world now rearranged,
as on we spiral into the years ahead,
each taking us farther away
into what the future will say.

These anniversaries will come again
with their memories and their pain,
but, maybe, the first blow landed
will make way for fond remembrance again,
and other first times,
they are sure to come,
but none like this,
not this first one.

80.

Sometimes I wonder, why bother? With Joe's dying, I realize how little I have to say about what happens. Not that I want these thoughts, but they intrude, forcing their way into my thinking. I route them out, but sometimes not at first, indulging them for awhile before they are banished. But go they must, and they will, for there is no future there. I will bother as always for there is still meaning to be had. So much of it came from Joe.

Bothering
(February 21, 2003)

Why bother?
From whence and where do these thoughts appear,
in these words whose voice do I hear?
Is it you, Despair,
seeking new prey,
new hopes, new dreams for you to slay,
in pursuit seeing I am weakened?
Yes, I am down,
Yes, I am holding on,
but I have strength enough for you.

Begone, Despair!
You are not wanted here,
you with no future, with no past,
no field to sow but tragedy,
prying free the grip of hope,
another captive to join your descent
to nowhere.

OH JOE!

No, Despair,
I am here and here I stay,
daring to bother with another day,
and you, you go on alone,
foiled again by the bothering to be done.

81.

I still find myself in the midst of pain that at times seems too much. My mind still struggles to grasp Joe's dying. It takes all my effort to comprehend it. Somewhere in the recesses of my mind, there is a belief system that tells me I can go on. I will survive. It can offer no sense to be made, no explanations, only constructs of meaning and context of happening. However much or little, this is something. Perhaps it is all there is in trying to come to terms with Joe's death. I believe it is there and will lead me on to whatever awaits me. I cannot get there now. I am caught up in too much. All I can do is feel and hurt. I have not been able to make room for hope and promise. They will come. I believe it. When they do, I will be ready.

Tucked Away
(February 21, 2003)

There is tucked away
in a place far, far away
a belief to be had and held
to lead me on,
to welcome me back to the living,
returning me to the world.
I cannot see it from here,
but have been told of its coming
if I can hold out til then.

For now,
the emotions are too raw,
they hurt to the touch,
crowding out too much,
but I know it is there,
this belief that leads me on,
still beyond my reach,
but waiting ahead somewhere,
not to be rushed,
patient until I can feel my way there.

82.

It is said the pain will ease with time. Things will get better. At times, it seems they are. Then, without warning, memories are triggered. The truth is driven home. The pain is even greater. It might be a sight, a sound, a passing remark, some reminder of Joe, and it all comes rushing back. Nothing is the same. It will never be again. Time cannot change it. Time can only do so much. Perhaps we expect too much.

Getting Worse
(February 27, 2003)

How can it be getting worse
after all this time?
Not that it was better,
but at least not worse,
there was the beginning of hope.

Suddenly,
with the vengeance of a job not yet done,
it grows again,
the sense of loss, the loss of Joe,
lying in wait, biding its time,
and I am overcome,
driven deeper and deeper down,
desperate to find a haven
not to be found,
unarmed,
unable to ward off the sadness
arrived unwarned.

It is bleak out there,
bleak in here,
and cold.

OH JOE!

Life has slipped away,
and I am forever chilled
day after day.

83.

Death forces us to confront the concept of meaning. When it occurs at its expected time or place, or close to it, we speak of "meaning," but do not look too closely because it was going to happen. It is a part of life, its unfolding and its ending. Other times, death cries out to be understood when it strikes unannounced and devastates with its cruelty. So it was with Joe. I struggle to make some sense of it all, to find some meaning to console me and give me hope. So far, there is none. In my head, I can rationalize, but not here in my heart. It is still so wounded, I wonder if it will ever heal. I recoil at the thought of trying to find meaning in this, as if anything could explain why it had to be, why now, why Joe.

Meaning
(February 27, 2003)

Our wonder at meaning is so often
so sparing,
unneeded for the slights and jolts
that do not matter,
we can go on,
the changes are just enough,
we are slowed, sometimes stopped,
though not for long,
when we have our way we are entitled.
What is there to ask?

Even death has a pace,
hard to take but bearing down
and we know its coming,
until it is out of turn,
ruthless invader who does not warn,
seizing before its time for taking,
leaving behind those left quaking,
left in pain with questions why,
and unfinished dreams left to die,

looking for answers not to be found,
some sign of meaning nowhere around.

And I forced back at last
from whence I came,
into the hands of God held out the same,
back for there is nowhere else to go,
the meaning will be there
if there is meaning to know,
the meaning and more,
for it is there I will find Joe.

84.

Peggy made a comment that put it well: People do not like to be around depressed people. They can only stand so much depression. Then, they do not call, or visit, or ask anymore. They wait for us to call when what we need is prompting to coax us back to life. Desperate for their attention, we pretend so they will stay, as much as we can, not saying what we need said, not voicing what we need to hear, until we are up to it no longer and withdraw. But even with so much left unshared, their presence, their voices, the notes they write, help.

Don't Leave
(February 27, 2003)

I peer out at familiar faces
looking back at who
they think they know,
who I used to be.
I want to keep them here,
but they will not linger with strangers,
and so I muffle my cries,
I can only cry out for so long,
they can only take so much
before taking flight.

As much as I need
I do without,
grateful for the least they have to give,
I will take anything,
and so in one last reach
to keep them here,
summoning all my reserve,
I smile,
and hope it is enough.

85.

In so many ways, I feel I am in another life. Try as I might, my life, my world, is not the same. This is not to say it does not go on, only that it does so differently. I do not yet have my bearings. I have been changed, but I do not know in what ways or how much, or what it will mean for what I will choose to do. For now, I will do the same as I have always done, trying to fashion a way to live in an altered world. Joe did not leave me alone. He left his imprint on me, and I will honor it in all that I do.

Another Life
(March 1, 2003)

I find myself in another life,
a stranger in a foreign land.
I see signs I have been here before,
remnants of the old,
recollections return,
landmarks fade in and out,
familiar faces, known places,
but hardly recognizable,
the past out of focus,
like eyeglasses out of date,
ahead, darkened outlines of an eclipse
that will not wait.

I am somewhere in between,
my feet not yet planted,
the ground not yet firm,
stepping gingerly, testing the way,
hesitant to put my weight,
fearing to seal my fate,
feeling my way in the dark,
a child again learning to walk.

OH JOE!

Is there only the sinister void ahead,
and I, in between, wondering,
How much is alive?
How much is dead?

86.

It is Joe's birthday, March 4, 2003. The first since he died. The feelings overwhelm me. It was only one year ago that we sat here, all of us, in this house to celebrate. The world seemed so big and beautiful. It was open before us. So much was going on. There was so much to do. We had such plans. We could not know it would be his last. Thank God for this not knowing. We must be thankful for small blessings.

First Birthday
(March 4, 2003)

Joe's birthday is here,
the first since his leaving,
and so are we,
closeted inside these walls
with pictures and pain,
videos and voice again,
images of Joe last year,
the last year Joe was here.

The celebration returns
in colors and shapes from then,
taking residence with us again,
Joe still here within these walls,
safe from the world's heartless calls,
and we with him if we will stay
behind these walls on this his day,
behind these walls where Joe resides,
having nothing to do with the world outside.

87.

A new feeling has come over me since Joe died, pulling me in two directions, wanting to stay with those left here, wanting to go on with Joe. There is much to do and I look forward to its doing; but there is not the same fear and dread of when I must go for Joe waits for me ahead. Others are there, too, but their going was easier to see as their appointed time. Not Joe. His was unexpected. He was not ready. I was not ready. I am torn between the two, the going and the staying, desperately wanting to stay, but not as afraid to go.

Fear of Death
(March 8, 2003)

I fear death less now,
not that I am looking to go
though I long to see Joe,
but between the wanting and the waiting
there is much to do,
much to turn my attention to,
and I will while I can
with less dread when the ebbing comes,
more ready to leave now when my day is done,
mourning those I will leave in the past,
my mourning for Joe then ended at last.

88.

Sometimes my mind plays tricks on me, tempting me with thoughts that Joe is not gone. I want to believe it and, sometimes, do not dismiss it right away. I indulge the thought. Where is the line between consciousness and dream or some state in between? Could I be there? How much of what we see is illusion, driven and shaped by the needs of our minds? How much can be denied? How much proof do we need? And so I let the trick go on, though I know better, thinking, if only for a moment, maybe it is not a trick.

Tricks
(March 10, 2003)

My mind still plays tricks on me,
hinting this is just a dream,
taking me out of time,
taking me back,
slowing the march without Joe,
so relentless, so uncaring,
stopping the world for a moment
as I catch my breath.

I do not trust what I see.
How much is missed?
How much mistaken?
It is all so unreal,
maybe it is.

And then the signs everywhere appear,
heartless testimony to my fears,
Joe is gone no longer here,
I can only miss him in my tears.

89.

Sometimes I lie in bed awake, not yet moved to rise. Looking ahead to the day, it dawns on me again that Joe is gone. How I wish to avoid facing it. How easy it would be to stay under the covers, to pass on the day and close it out. If I could just stay here, I would not have to join in a world that has taken Joe. I will not have to go on without him. Maybe his death will seem less real. I can be alone here with my memories. Sometimes its helps to put it off by staying here beneath the covers.

The Covers
(March 12, 2003)

Here again I lay
under the comfort of the covers,
silent refuge, cloistered away,
my world shrinking to this,
where I can be alone with thoughts of Joe,
the world out there kept out,
kept away from Joe in here,
here where we laugh and talk as we once did,
in this silent world safely hid.

Even here I am sad,
for there are no plans for the future,
no future to be had,
only a place to visit and return again
to relive for a moment how we were then.

There is safety in these covers,
or so it seems,
this tender place where dreams
can still be dreamed.

90.

I feel emptiness so much of the time. I try to engage, but the effort falls short. Too much has been taken. Too much is wounded and has not yet healed. I am left searching for what I feel, finding it hard to put words to. But I can try.

The Hollowing
(March 15, 2003)

Joe is gone,
and I am less,
hollowed out by the sweep of Life
and its takings,
first one, then another, and now Joe,
sometimes fearing there is nothing left to defend.

Hope has taken flight,
darkness has taken over light,
stealing away while on I tried,
without a word as on I cried,
leaving me wounded and bare,
nothing to hold to for there is nothing there.

But I place my trust that just beyond
there is hope for me to be found,
where belief lives on and promise waits,
and I stand poised at its gates,
left there by all who have gone
for me to follow,
gifts to me to fill the hollow,
making their places with me
as I make my way,
with courage to face another day,
filling me with enough to live,
enough of living left for me to give.

91.

It is the early morning hours again, not yet light. I am in a hotel room on a business trip. Suddenly, I was awake, though I do not recall waking. It was black all around at first. Then, slowly, I began to make out shapes, not recognized as anything yet, but no longer one shade of black. They emerged more and more, defined by what I knew was there and not yet by seeing. I thought, this is much like my life has been since Joe's passing. Darkness all around and me responding more to shapes and what I expect them to be. Life is no longer as well known as before. It is less recognizable, but still familiar enough to get by as I redefine who I am, where I am.

Shapes
(March 19, 2003)

I wake to black
when the waking is sudden,
as my eyes slowly adjust to the dark,
different shades
where I can make out only shapes,
they could be anything,
my mind races and roams
seeking some level,
a glimmer of recognition.

There is a void out there
in the blackness,
in the unknown,
as waking slowly scatters sleep away,
and my mind fills in the details.
I know where I am,
or where I was,
but in that first instant of blackness,
in the vacuum,
it is like starting over,
starting anew,

but there is no new start for me,
nothing to make Joe's passing untrue.

Sometimes the darkness is easier,
staying here,
shunning the light where Joe cannot be seen,
holding on to shapes and imaginings
where he might be.

This darkness follows me into day,
into a world where I see only shapes,
outlines of what used to be,
nothing as distinct as I used to see,
as the days get shorter,
the shapes blur on,
and I live more on habit
to do what must be done.

92.

Springtime came again this year, with budding greens and colors flowering in vivid shades not yet faded by the sun, life renewing itself. I have always loved Springtime, but not as much this year. It is not as full or rich without Joe here. I think of last year when Spring and the world were as they should be, the colors and the changes touching me. I felt them inside. Not now. They reach to me the same, call upon my senses, but I am not as attuned to what they say. My head nods in recognition, but they glance off my heart. Things are so different now. How do I reconstruct the world so I can enter it again? Joe's hand must guide me. His voice will tell me. I must listen.

First Spring
(February 21, 2003)

I love Springtime,
the burst of new life,
the greening and the flowering,
colors so vivid,
hues not yet faded from heat
and dried from thirst,
but I cannot love it as much this year,
for all the newness and renewal,
there is not as much life this time here.

I see it all about me,
can recall how I felt,
but not how it feels,
I am detached,
a mere observer with nothing more to say
than a blank page.

I know what to feel,
can say it out loud,
but the sensation eludes me,
it is over there somewhere

and I am here
outside the cadence of life,
feeling only the loss of Joe.

Nothing drowns it out or makes it less,
nor do I want it to,
I will hold it forever,
knowing that slowly it will nurse me
back to health,
leading me into the world again,
for Joe's hand is written there,
writ to me,
telling me I must care.

93.

One day driving to work after stopping by the cemetery, I thought of how life goes on and, in its going, takes me with it. Its pull is exerted first in demands, things that must be done. Then, widening its appeal, it holds out choices that can be taken or left. At first, they are left. Then, little by little, some are taken. Each draws me back into life again. This is what Joe wants. It is his way of releasing his hug around me, but never letting go. His hand will always be there, on my shoulder, in my hand, and, when I need it, his arms will surround me again until I am ready to stand alone. Yes, Joe, you will always be with me. With this, I can carry on.

The Beckoning
(March 21, 2003)

I see a beckoning out there,
signs of life enticing me to return,
drawing me back with demands and promises,
Time the author of it all,
reminding there is only now
and I am here.

"Come back! Come back!"
they say,
as I look into their eyes,
and then look back,
wanting to stay,
freezing Time if I could,
but feeling all the while
Joe pushing me to go.

"Go on! Go on!" he says,
for I go with you
in all the memories that I gave,
memories of us for you to save,
I am with you always, always near,

as you are with me even here,
and so I will answer the beckoning's call,
answer it for Joe,
knowing he will be with me
through it all.

94.

Sometimes there are good days. I do not know how or why they arrive. They come unannounced, but are welcome when they do. Those days, the world looks better. I feel more hopeful. Colors are brighter. Things look more familiar. I am more at home with the world around me. Then, suddenly, it can strike and the good day is gone. It might be a face, a place, a picture, anything to trigger a memory of Joe, and I am down, at least for a while. All memories do not do this. More and more, they are grateful remembrances that do not compete with the world that is left or resist my efforts to rejoin it. Others linger and bring back images and dreams lost that cut to the quick, and I am sad. They are fragile, these good days. Hopefully, they will become more hardy as time goes by.

The Good Days
(March 21, 2003)

The good days are so fragile when they come,
lifting the gloom,
allowing sparks of joy and hope
to rush in,
as they wait for the chance,
moments so rare,
they are savored,
knowing they will soon go,
but each time their stay will be longer,
until they have a home with me again.

Suddenly, sometimes,
they are swept away in an instant,
it takes no more than a face, a place, a memory,
these, too, treasured and dear
but piercing reminders that Joe is not near,
and for those moments, and in those thoughts,
all my hoping and joying is brought to naught,
leaving only my grief that Joe is gone,
and my waiting for the next good day to come.

95.

I still find Joe's death hard to believe. I go about the days, make my plans, mix with others, but they can keep me from thought only so long. It still seems unreal. After all this time, it is no easier to accept. If I think of what has happened, how can this be? I know it is, but how? Why? I am still asking. I think I always will.

Disbelief
(March 25, 2003)

Each day I wake in disbelief
that Joe has died
and must believe it all over again.
I pray it was a dream, a nightmare,
anything but true,
always hoping to wake to the world
I knew,
sometimes seeming I almost do,
in those twilight moments before sleep is gone,
that middle ground where anything can be done,
and then that haven, too, slips away,
and I once again face a world unmade,
questioning anew if it has happened,
able to believe it only for awhile
before my mind wonders again
and wanders lost in a wilderness it does not know.
It is so hard to live in a world of disbelief.

96.

I sense life returning in me in stages, little bits here and there. Sometimes I still resist. I do not want to let go. Of what? Not memories, for they will stay. I will treasure them forever. There will be stories of Joe told and told again. We are already able to laugh sometimes as we cry. It is God and Joe at work here. God is turning back over to me more and more of the load He has been carrying. And Joe, I can feel his hand and hug bidding me to go on, wishing me well, assuring me he will be with me along the way. Still, I feel guilty for going on. Maybe this, too, will pass.

In Stages
(March 29, 2003)

I smiled today for awhile,
and felt it in ways not felt before,
basking in the feeling like the sun's glow,
until I forced it away,
uneasy lest I enjoy too much,
not yet ready for that,
but easier than yesterday.

They creep back in,
these feelings I remember from so long ago,
feelings left with Joe,
as he returns them to me,
little by little,
with his blessing.

There is God's hand, too,
as He slowly shifts more of the load and life
back to me,
not too much, not too fast,
but in stages,
like the terms of a peace agreement,
knowing better than I

OH JOE!

it is time, I am ready,
my strength returning,
the world pulsing with life
and my pulse quickening again.

97.

I lie in bed sometimes, awake, eyes shut, as if I can keep the world out. Maybe then I can avoid the truth out there that Joe has died. Is this my last, my only refuge? What does it matter? It does not last. But if it brings even a moment's relief, the slightest escape, how I need it.

Eyes Shut
(April 5, 2003)

My eyes are shut,
and I, shuttered inside,
as if the world out there will not find me,
or can not reach me here,
flailing away as it may out there,
I am outside its grasp in here,
safe because I cannot see it,
but the escape does not hold,
the images seep in,
warring for my attention,
circling, no mercy.

Every memory I flee hovers out there
and reaches behind the lids in here,
laying claim to my peace,
forcing the truth upon me,
until, my eyes opening again,
I am released
into the wild once more,
into this tortured land not seen before.

98.

It was a long weekend in Destin. It was good to get away. I needed the break. Lying in bed one morning, I thought of all the pretending that goes on. I do my job, act the part, go on as I must, but things are not the same. They are so wrong. Joe is not here. Sometimes I need an escape from the pretense to feel what I feel without interruption or demand. I need this time away.

Pretending
(April 6, 2003)

On I go
in my tries to go on,
all falling short,
like pretending Joe is not gone,
retracing steps taken before,
but all walked when Joe was here,
not new and yet not the same this year.
What are they? Who am I?

Sometimes the pretense is too much
and I must stop, a break,
going neither forward nor backward,
staying still so nothing more will change,
nothing to carry me farther away,
allowing me to rest until
I am ready to pretend again,
waiting as I do for the day
when the motions and the acting
are no longer pretending as before,
but me alive again once more.

99.

As I go about rejoining the world, part of me is kept back in time when Joe was here. I never left. Though I venture out in my new surroundings, I can leave Joe's world for only so long. I return to it as much as it seeks me out for I miss Joe and it is there I can find him. He is here, too, I know, in my thoughts and memories. But he seems more real if I can visit back then.

Kept Back
(April 29, 2003)

As I venture farther
into my new surroundings,
part of me is kept back
tending to the true reality
when Joe was here,
not this pretender I see about me,
assuring me life goes on.

There is life left out of this
unreal world that lingers on,
and I must tend to that life too,
as this part of me kept back will do,
this part that stays with Joe alive,
this staying needed for me to survive.

100.

I have written of how I have gone through the motions of life since Joe died, my heart not in it, the effort forced. Over time, I find, the forcing begins to take on the aspect of habit, gone through without as much consciousness. Perhaps this is the only way to go on. Even then, the truth breaks through: Joe is not here. I realize again how much is not there that used to be and how much forcing this takes from me.

Missing
(May 2, 2003)

Sometimes the illusion will not hold,
for all the forcing,
all the effort turned to habit,
the escape from consciousness,
there is a break in the acting,
truth intrudes and descends
darkening my world like an eclipse,
Joe is gone.

Everything falls short for he is missing,
an emptiness I try and do not want to fill,
surfacing in a sight, a sound, perhaps a place,
or sometimes nothing I can say,
until a sliver of light appears
signaling the return of day,
and I press on,
making the best of what is in store,
hoping in time it will matter more.

101.

This morning, like so many mornings, I thought back to this time last year when Joe was here. All I can think or feel is that Joe was here and now is gone. My heart breaks again. How can I be in this moment without him? It is so incomplete. I should be back then.

Thinking Back
(May 9, 2003)

It is so hard thinking back
to this time last year
when Joe was here.

We went our way
as if we owned each passing day,
and we did,
or did not know better,
or at least not when,
the memories so special now
that they are all we have.

But wondrous then, too,
as memories were made in all we'd do,
the specialness there though unspoken,
well understood by a heart not yet broken,
and now the heartbreak and the longing,
they come with such a cost,
but a price well paid
for what was lost.

Thinking back,
how I want not to leave,
but leaving I must,
left now only to grieve.

102.

My efforts to go on only go so far. I can feel better, but only so much, for only so long. The pain returns. It is never truly gone. I may be distracted for a time, occupied for a while, but it does not last. I have been wounded, and it is grave. I will survive, but the wounding goes on.

The Wounding
(May 29, 2003)

Life has such a wounding way
with its piercings and its takings,
not deadly until the end
but what a toll until then,
wounding me in taking Joe,
a wounding hold that does not let go.

My spirit limps,
my steps slowed, more measured now,
taking measure of what is gone and how,
Time not long or cure enough to heal
or change what is forever real,
like a stigmata the pain returns
reminding how much is yearned.

Through the bindings of Life
that doctor me,
through all the prayers to comfort me,
the Past forces its way in
as Life's wounding way wounds again.

103.

I think back a year ago when Joe died. Life was good. Joe had just moved into his new house four months earlier. He was to be married in two weeks. He was at the top of his job. He had just competed in a national bodybuilding competition in Philadelphia three weeks before he entered the hospital. Then this. Unknown. Unforeseen. Out of nowhere. Will I ever feel safe again?

The Lulling
(June 10, 2003)

How easily we are lulled
when all is well.
Sleep is sound, dawn is fresh,
the black of night not so fearsome,
unable, unwilling to doubt
lest it come true.

How tempting to believe it will last,
as now turns into past,
knowing deep inside
there are limits to the ride,
but far off in another time,
not near enough for me to mind.

Then suddenly far off is here,
facing me in trembling fear,
and then the deadly deed is done,
Life has claimed another one,
Life this time has claimed my son,
no lulling left in its wake,
no more lulling I can take,
and another loss follows me
from where I've been,
knowing I will never be lulled again.

104.

I am told a year has passed since Joe died. The calendar, the changes in the seasons, a year's worth of my comings and goings, tell me it is true. But in my heart, no time has passed at all. On this day, June 28, I am still there in the hospital room, feeling my last touch of Joe, holding him in my final hug, seeing my last look at his life, saying my last good-bye, giving him my final kiss. The pain is as real now as it was then. The loss is just as deep. The hurt seems without end. How can I bear it? Oh, Joe!

One Year
(June 28, 2003)

It has been a year they say
since Joe died,
and I have no way to argue,
the signs are all about,
but meant for someone else,
Time has left me out,
left me here with Joe at the end,
holding fast to my last grasp of him,
as if I could relax my hold
and leave him in a world gone cold.

He holds me, too,
in tugs and pulls upon my heart
neither Time nor Life can keep apart.
We are fixed in time on that day,
we two,
in those last moments of the life we knew,
moments that must last a lifetime
until I can share his new life, too.

105.

It is the day after the anniversary of Joe's death. They say it takes a year to get over a loss like this. In the first year, we experienced everything for the first time without Joe. We could look back to the same time last year, and Joe was there. It was a time with him. This was our memory of the year before. The first year has now passed, and I am more down than ever. Now, when I look back on last year, I see a year when Joe was not here. A year without him has been forced between us. It will only get worse. The next years will do it, too, punishing proof that Life has gone on without him. How can this be? How can I face it? It is one thing to take one day at a time as I have done this first year. To look back on the whole year at once forces the reality of Joe's dying upon me all over again. It is almost more real and harder to bear. How did I survive it? Facing the next year ahead and the years like them to come is as shattering as ever. I know no years can take my memories of Joe. I can fight the distance. But to not be able to look back on last year and see a year with Joe in it, I have lost something more. Less of me is left. A part has stayed in this last year, taking residence in the memories. It is there this part of me belongs.

Next Year
(June 29, 2003)

The first year is done,
the next awaits,
and I do not want to go,
for more than the first year is gone,
taken, too,
is my last look at last year
when Joe was here.

In my looks back then
I could see Joe again,
as we lived and laughed
and saw no end,
Time had not yet come between,
the first year had not intervened.
Now, these first year looks are taken, too,

OH JOE!

Time determined to force me through,
no looks back left to last year with Joe,
only last year without him
and years to go.

I will not be taken easily.
No, part of me will not go,
will stay with the memories
of this last year with Joe
this part of me that does not go on,
but stays with Joe where I belong.

As for the rest,
I will press on into the years ahead,
into the chapters planned for me unread,
and looking back the memories,
they will remain,
but, no longer last year,
they are not the same.
No, there is new pain and loss
in these next years,
but this pain, too,
will keep Joe near.

What Is There To Say?

What is there to say? I have tried to say it here. Still, after all is said and done, I am left alone. Bereft. Struggling for hope. Searching for purpose. My prayers mixed, to feel better, to not let go. And the sadness, the endless, searing sorrow that wakens me each day, and so grudgingly lets go each night. It will be there tomorrow. It always is. I will cry when it comes and when it leaves and off and on in between until the next day when it starts again. What is there to say? Nothing more than, from deep within my hurting heart, from the depths of my grieving soul, "Oh Joe!"

But there is more. From the depths, I hear a voice. It is the voice that assured St. Paul as he suffered, "My grace is enough for you" (2 Corinthians 12: 9); that calmed the disciples in the boat during the storm, "Do not be afraid" (Matthew 14: 27); that promised His followers, "I will not leave you orphaned" (John 14: 18); that comforted the apostles before His death, "Do not let your hearts be troubled. Have faith in God and faith in me" (John 14: 1); and whose last words before ascending to the Father were, "And know that I am with you always, until the end of the world" (Matthew 28: 20).

And there is another voice. It is Joe, calling to me, "Hey, Dad." He is still here. In the depths. Across the divide. Always.

0-595-66032-0

Printed in the United States
144267LV00004B/9/A